Miss Your FOREVER

REFLECTIONS AFTER THE DEATH OF A SPOUSE

DOMINIC MURGIDO

ISBN 978-1-0980-6946-9 (paperback)
ISBN 978-1-0980-6947-6 (digital)

Christian Faith Publishing, Inc.
832 Park Avenue
Meadville, PA 16335
www.christianfaithpublishing.com

Printed in the United States of America

To my wife, Susan. She was my best friend who loved dark chocolate and shopping for a bargain, quick with a witty remark, always fun to be with, and there for anyone in need. She touched so many lives that have been forever changed by her kindness and compassion. Her spirit lives within me.

Contents

II

III

IV

Preface

None of us know what tomorrow will be, so let's not take the present for granted.

I am a regular guy who fell in love in college and was married a month after graduation. I was blessed and felt pretty good about the life I was beginning personally and professionally.

During our lives together, my wife and I moved many times due to my job, and each move brought its challenges as well as us growing closer together. We celebrated life with vacations and trips and had a beautiful daughter. My wife, Susan (who liked me to call her Susie), was always there for me, encouraging, inspiring, and loving.

Susie was a planner, big time. There was a point that she had our vacation plans five years out, marking special *anniversaries* and *birthdays*. I wasn't complaining. Any time with her was always fun no matter where we were or what we were doing.

Life was good. All was well. We were happy.

Then the unexpected happened. She was killed when a truck was speeding and ran a red light and struck her vehicle as she was driving through an intersection. She died instantly. I died a little that day too.

This is where my story begins.

Introduction

Grief is as individual as one's fingerprint. We all deal with things differently, and it all depends on how it happened and where you were in the period of your life with your loved one when the unfortunate happens to you. This is my story, and it is how I felt and continue to feel and deal with the tragedy that was mine. I realize and am very thankful that I had the means to make change happen for me that others could not do under the same circumstance, and for that, I am grateful. Change is something that I talk about a lot on these pages. Change is good. Change is inevitable.

This is a collection of thoughts and feelings that I have experienced since the death of my wife. In addition to my thoughts and feelings on these pages, some became articles that I wrote for newsletters as well as reproductions of actual entries from my personal journal as I wrote them along the way. Yes, I did journal. Not that I knew I was doing so in the beginning, but after a year of writing thoughts on three-by-five cards, I was told that's what it was. I also included a time line of my grieving process to further explain what I went through. Everyone going through this grieving process will have a different time line.

It is my intention to share with the reader what I experienced and felt after the death of my wife. These are my thoughts and feelings, and it is my hope that sharing will help others realize that they are not alone on their grief journey.

Too often, grief—and all that surrounds you during your bereavement process—can be very isolating. There are times that there is no one that understands where you are coming from or where you are going, including yourself. I strongly recommend attending a grief support group as well as seek counseling and therapy to help you get your life back on track without forgetting your past.

That's what I did.

I

Her Last Birthday

Life was good. Still in love and to be married to a wonderful woman, Sue, who was also my best friend. It couldn't get any better. But unknown to me and anyone, my life as I knew it was about to be turned upside down, while her life here was about to end.

Sue had a commitment on her birthday, January 13, that began her day, and it involved her dog, *Hal.*

Hal and Sue were scheduled for a visit to the local assisted-living facility near our home. Hal was trained as a therapy dog, and he and Sue would spend time together visiting those less fortunate in settings such as this as well as other locations where people looked forward to such a visit from a friendly pair as they were. Sue was also part of a therapy dog group that would involve multiple dogs and their handlers visiting facilities to put on a group demo and show to entertain the residents. Together, Sue and Hal would bring a little sunshine and a smile to others.

Our plans for the day started with a tour of the Wolfgang Chocolate Company, located in York, Pennsylvania. Neither one of us had ever been there. Sue, being the chocoholic that she was, was excited to be doing this especially on her birthday. Unfortunately, I read the tour times wrong, and their only tours were given twice a day at specific times. We missed the morning one, and the afternoon one wasn't until hours later, so we decided to continue on with our day and maybe stop back in the afternoon while we were on our way home. As we were about to leave, one of the women behind the counter of the gift shop came out to us as we were exiting into the parking lot and said that she would take us on an individual tour (just the two of us). We were both like children in the delight of not only being able to take a tour but all by ourselves. It was so nice of that woman to do this for us, being Sue's birthday and all.

At the conclusion of the tour, we learned something neither of us knew—a favorite candy of Sue's was actually produced there. The company from another town trucked their chocolate to this company where this company actually made it for them. We saw the molds and were convinced the tour guide was correct, a fun fact that we came to know from the tour that we enjoyed solo.

The rest of our day was shopping and lunch of course at a small deli in Hanover, Pennsylvania. I was never much of a shopper, but over the years, I became a bargain hunter like my wife. We would see which of us could get the better deal of the day, often bragging for days about it. Sue had a way to make anything you did with her fun.

The rest of the weekend was the usual, having-stuff-to-do-around-the-house kind of thing for us. On Sunday, the fifteenth, Sue and a good friend went shopping for most of the day.

Our Sunday nights usually concluded with watching *60 Minutes* and *The Amazing Race* and the devouring of cookies and milk or cookies and tea. Sue was a tea lover, and I'd even go to say somewhat of a connoisseur.

Her Final Day

It was the third Monday of a new year. It was Martin Luther King Jr. Day. It was the sixteenth of January 2006. And like any other day, it began the same and continued on its course in a familiar way.

I left for work after a goodbye kiss, and she more than likely followed suit in her routine of planning her morning of errands, including a walk with her best friend, Hal, her blue merle sheltie on a wooded trail near the house. She wasn't due at work till two that afternoon.

I was in a meeting at work all of the morning and, by early afternoon, was in my office when the phone rang. On the other end was her boss, owner of a local pharmacy. This was the pharmacy that Sue worked at. He called to ask about Sue. She had not come into work, and his efforts to reach her were getting nowhere. We had a brief conversation, concluding that she must have gotten ill and is not picking up the home phone or her cell phone.

I told him I would get back to him and left work to go home to check on Sue's whereabouts. At home, all was well as it should be. Her car was gone, the house was locked up as it should, and our dog Hal was there being Hal. I then surmised that she probably was on her way to work and had car trouble and probably had no cell service to call. I thought I would take the route she takes to work to find her, a route I never knew about until her birthday three days ago when she showed me a different way home from our day out using the reverse of her usual route to work.

I came across a fire policeman ahead that was redirecting traffic to the left. As I pulled up to him and rolled my window down, I asked what was happening. He told me there had been an accident, and there was a fatality. I broke down in tears, knowing that the fatality was my wife. I don't know how or why this happened to me, but it proved out to be true.

After he called someone on the radio, I was asked to proceed ahead. Shortly down the road was an accident scene that was to haunt me for many years.

Fire trucks, rescue squads, police vehicles were everywhere. Traffic cones, glowing flares, caution tape, flashing lights, and scores of first responders were all over the intersection.

I was in the middle of a sea of disruption, chaos, fear, and uncertainty. I was alone even though surrounded by dozens of people I never met before. The looks on their faces immediately told me the story I did not want to hear. Life, as I loved it and knew it, was about to change forever, and there was nothing I could do to prevent it. After hearing it directly from a police officer, I crumpled to the ground as a lost soul in a world I was no longer familiar with.

Dealing with My Loss

Writing about my grief journey began within days of my wife's death when I began to write on three by five cards in the middle of the night when I couldn't sleep. Writing about what I felt is something I never did before except in a letter or a greeting card to my wife. This was so new to me, and eventually, I wrote in and completed journals of my thoughts and what I was feeling. None of what I wrote had to be shared with anyone. Writing in a journal was a safe place to share my thoughts without being judged. I found it comforting to be able to just write exactly how I felt—good or bad. There is something about putting thoughts down on paper through the instrument of a pen that allows one to be relieved of some of the sadness and anxiety that you feel as it is happening. This writing in a journal eventually was an every-night ritual right before I went to bed at the end of the day.

Within four to six weeks after the death of my wife, I know I needed help—help to cope, understand, be well, continue to live. I sought out a bereavement support group that was operated by a local hospital. This group was for anyone that was suffering from the loss of a loved one, and it was one night a week for six weeks.

I didn't know what to expect or anything about what I was to get involved with, but I knew that I needed something to get me on track or to feel like I wasn't alone in all of this. There were about ten people there, men and women, all going through the loss of a loved one—mothers, fathers, husbands, wives, sisters, brothers. We were all there to seek help and feel better in some way.

There is so much to be said about this kind of setting, a group of strangers sitting in a common place with common heartache, talking and listening and feeling the compassion that you need to receive. This incredible bond just happens among those that are in attendance. This group, although informal, was structured in some ways with an agenda for each week. It included handouts and guest speakers and was facilitated by a nun who was the chaplain of the local hospital.

After the first meeting, I wasn't sure I belonged there and doubted the help this could provide for me, but I continued to attend. After the third week, I was feeling comfortable and a little bit better about my feelings and emotions. There was one man there that lost his wife in a sudden unexpected accident, and I found myself drawn to him. We'd talk after the meetings a little and had so many similar feelings about this kind of loss of a spouse.

After the sixth week, the support group concluded. I did feel better, but I needed more. I started to seek out and eventually found a therapist to help me one on one. This was very helpful to me. I met with the therapist weekly to start and, eventually, every other week, then monthly. I always felt a little better each time I left their office. Talking with a professional counselor or therapist about your feelings and issues is a great way to express and help yourself maintain a sense of being in the present.

The therapist was helping me cope with and think about where I was in life now without my wife. I continued this for many years but missed the group experience and sharing with others. The therapist encouraged me to seek out another group to attend.

I called the facilitator of the group I attended, and she provided me a phone number of another group. I called, and this general bereavement support group met monthly and was designed to never end. It was ongoing, and you could come and go as you needed to. It was free and no registration required. The downside was that it was about an hour drive from my house. I knew that I needed this kind of help through a group in addition to the personal therapy sessions, so I began to attend this bereavement support group.

I went to this support group and once again found myself in a setting that was beneficial to me. I continued to attend this group monthly, getting to know and understand others going through their grief journey. There were some people in attendance that lost their spouse suddenly and unexpectedly like I did. I noticed the same bond I experienced before was happening all over again. Being part of a grief support group and sharing among those that have similar feelings and emotions is safe and comforting.

While attending this support group, it became apparent to me that attending a bereavement support group that was specific to the loss would be better for me, such as one that dealt with the loss of spouse or significant other. I would begin a search to locate one.

Everyone that attended this group brought their feelings to the table, and there wasn't any judgment among us. I remember after one meeting, the facilitator of the group approached me and gave me a copy of a bereavement newsletter she subscribed to with an article in it about something I was saying in a past meeting.

After reading the article, I felt like it really helped to validate my feelings and where I was on my journey. I wrote to the publication to express my gratitude for the article and began an email exchange with the editor, who encouraged me to tell my story in an article.

Months later, I did just that. I wrote an article entitled "Her Spirit Lives within Me" and submitted it to the editor of that newsletter. The article was published in December 2007. That was the first time my thoughts in writing were seen by anyone other than the pages of my journal.

The article was well received, and I continued to write articles for that newsletter to share with their readers. This was the beginning of my writing for others to read in that newsletter and, eventually, was to begin my writing to be shared in my newsletter that I created in the fall of 2008. My newsletter began about six months after I created a bereavement support group for the sudden unexpected death of a spouse or significant other. The group is called *sudSSpirit*.

sudSSpirit is an acronym for: *s*udden *u*nexpected *d*eath of a *S*pouse *S*urvivors in *p*articipation to *i*nform, *r*enew, *i*mprove, and *t*riumph.

On the pages that follow will be reflections that I wrote to share with others through my newsletter and other newsletters since my wife died. There will also be a selection of entries from my personal journal that will follow the reflections. Most of the reflections and entries have appeared in the quarterly newsletter of *sudSSpirit*.

Reflections

Her Spirit Lives within Me

No one I ever met enjoys *Mondays*. It's the start of the work week, and in most cases, it comes after a relaxing enjoyable weekend. It's difficult to get motivated to begin the work week and continue through a Monday. Mondays will never be the same for me. They have become my greatest obstacle to overcome once a week. I actually renamed them Pre-Tuesday in my mind to help ease the anxiety I experience weekly.

It was Martin Luther King Jr. Day on *Monday*, January 16, 2006. As I began that day, I did not realize that my life would change forever in an instant. The instant came at 2:40 p.m. when I received a phone call from my wife's employer asking me if she was all right. Somewhat confused, I asked why and was told she did not come into work. She was scheduled at 2:00 p.m. that day. Efforts to contact her on the home phone and cell were fruitless. I drove home to check, and all looked fine as it should. I then thought that she was probably on the way to work and had gotten a flat tire and her cell wasn't getting a signal to call out.

I began to drive the route that she took to work to locate her, a route that she had just shown to me the previous Friday. I did locate her as being the *fatality* in a vehicle accident at an intersection where a tractor trailer ran a red light and broadsided her car. The truck pushed her car into a building where the structure partially collapsed. According to the coroner, she didn't know what hit her. She died instantly from blunt force trauma to the chest. I died a little that day too.

She was more than a wife to me and a mother to my daughter. She made me the man I am and was always there for me during struggles and successes. Most of my success as an individual I owe to her encouragement, love, and inspiration. I felt alone and as a victim by her departure from this life by a careless driver. My wife's forty-eighth birthday was three days prior to that fateful day.

We've known each other since we were eighteen and met at college. It was a beautiful relationship, marriage, and friendship, one that can never be duplicated because she certainly was *one in a million.*

My life without her continues to be painful at times, and perhaps there will always be a sadness that I experience and a hole in my heart. Our love was very strong, and I believe that the love we shared throughout our lives together is allowing me to feel her presence around me.

I am comforted with many wonderful memories and am constantly being reminded of our happy times together. It can be a song on the radio or a souvenir from a trip we were on or a special photograph of a place we had a good time together.

Any one event that brings a smile to my face, warmth to my heart, a reflection in my soul, makes me realize that she is with me, and I will never be without her spirit in my heart.

My Discovery of Journaling

If someone told me five years ago that I would journal someday, I would have looked at them like they were crazy. *Journaling* was something that did not appeal to me. Maybe it took a life-changing situation, like the sudden unexpected death of my wife, for my opinion to change on this topic.

Within days of my wife's passing, I found myself jotting down thoughts, fears, emotions, anger, regret, and confusion on three-by-five index cards. Each day, I would complete two or three cards with expressions of pain, frustration, and loneliness.

It is so common for those of us that have experienced the loss of a loved one to have feelings of hopelessness and helplessness. I found journaling to be a great release of my sadness and depression that I was experiencing with the knowledge that I was now without my wife. It also helped me with the struggle of so many unanswered questions concerning the rest of my life.

This daily ritual continued, and by the end of the first year, I completed about 250 cards. I received a journal of blank lined pages from someone as a gift. It was at that time I realized I was "journaling" and did not even realize it through my unrefined methods of utilizing simple three-by-five index cards.

Sometimes I would write a single word or only a few words to express my feelings. Other times I wrote incomplete sentences. Grammar, punctuation, and spelling did not matter when I wrote my thoughts and feelings. The content of what I was writing is what mattered. Depending on the time of year or the relevancy to a special date, there are many thoughts to reflect upon and write about. I date the entries and sometimes note the weather or a significant news item that is happening along with my thoughts. I reflect on things and how different it is without my wife being with me. I often comment on *"how she would say this or ask that"* if she were physically here with me or *"how much I miss that about her."*

My writings are not all sad; they also contain happy thoughts, memories, and even questions. There is something about writing down a question that makes it easier to deliberate the answer. And if you do not answer the question, it will be asked again on another day as you continue to write your thoughts. Eventually, you will answer it or resolve the conflict somehow.

I write daily, usually at the end of the day. I pick this time for the silence of the night and, in a way, as a ritualistic approach to going to bed alone, something that I am not used to doing. I find comfort in that time of day, pondering my thoughts and reducing my experiences to writing. I realize that putting my thoughts on paper allows me to vent, gives me a sense of peace, and provides me with an unofficial progress report at the same time.

Writings can be as simple as random thoughts jotted down that can become priceless months or years later as you process your experiences and feelings. I wrote for about a year and a half before I even thought about looking back at some of what I had already written in the past. I have never read all that I have written, nor do I go back regularly, just on occasion.

When you return to the past writings that you created, it allows you to see where you were and compare that to where you are now so that you can further understand where you are going. I read things that I wrote that I couldn't believe. It's amazing how you can believe in something at one time, and have another viewpoint on the same thing a month or so later. I also read some parts that made me cry all over again or smile at my humility. This process of writing can bring tears. There is nothing healthier than a good cry as you grieve your loved one.

Whatever works for you is what you do. Some people are more comfortable with a keyboard when expressing thoughts as an electronic "journal" on a computer. I began on index cards and expanded to an organized bound book form.

I continue to write with a pen on lined pages in a more traditional journal format. This form is best for me because it can be taken anywhere, and I am able to write anyplace. I find that when we think of things or experience an emotion as it relates to our bereavement, it is important to recognize it and jot it down. It may help us later or might mean something in the future as we continue to work through our grief journey.

When my wife died, my life and how I view the world has changed. This new world of mine is without her. I try to use my time of sorrow in order to grow as a new person through the journaling process. Journaling is for your benefit, and you can choose to keep it private to you. I encourage you to start and recognize how it can help you as it does for me.

Progress is something we all like to see in ourselves, especially in our own time of need. Our time of need combined with our grief experiences will yield with time. Be patient and allow yourself to heal.

So Many Memories, but It's Not the Same

When one loses a spouse, regardless of the reasons behind it, our lives change so much. We seem to go through the initial shock with some thought process about how different things will be for us. Little do we know that same feeling will reoccur again and again as time moves on. It will truly be hard to believe what has happened to us.

It has been said that when a loved one passes away, all that is left for the survivors are the memories. What's wrong with that? Memories, like a good book, can take you places. The cherished memories of the years you shared together take you to past times of fun, adventure, and pleasure with the one you loved. For a moment, you are there, and without realizing it, you begin to smile at the thought of the memory that you are recalling.

So many everyday situations can spur a memory of your loved one. You have to be open to the possibility that it can come at any time for you. It could be a phrase or an expression that you hear, or maybe someone's voice or laugh sounds similar to your spouse. I miss my wife's voice, her laugh, how she called the dog. Other situations can be a picture, a souvenir, a place, an event, a memento that you find or a place you visit that takes you back into the past of your lives together. Whatever it is, it's beautiful when it happens and must be regarded as being something very special that is happening to you.

My daily mundane routine has even changed or is experienced so differently now. I get up in the morning alone, eat breakfast alone, and that first cup of coffee in the morning is shared with no one anymore. I end my day alone. Conversation is lacking, reading articles in the paper to each other is no more. Taking walks, going out to dinner, attending an event we were invited to be at is now ignored because you would be doing it…alone.

It's not the same.

A year's time is filled with so many events, celebrations, holidays, birthdays, and anniversaries. You will, in time, be able to get through all of this as years go by. Some relatives and friends will remember you during that first year of grief, and that's nice. Other relatives and friends will continue to be in your new life every year, and that's even nicer. Things are different. They recognize it as you do.

Memories can be so ambivalent; they make us sad and happy at the same time. Memories help us recall how much we loved our wife or husband, how much we miss them, how lucky we were to have them be part of our life, and how much they contributed to us being the person we are today.

My marriage, in a sense, was my life. My life revolved around the unity of two people—myself and my spouse. When that unity was no more due to the loss of my wife, my life changed. I had no choice in the matter. I had to accept it. As part of the grieving process, you must come to terms with the death of your spouse. This is not easy to do. I think I am still trying to deal with this myself, even though it's been three years this month. There is no time limit with grief. It is what it is.

It's not the same.

The wedding vows that we had taken were so beautiful, symbolic, and represented the love and commitment that we wanted for one another. "To have and to hold from this day forward, for better or for worse, for richer, for poorer, in sickness and in health, to love and to cherish, until death do us part." I believe that the only parting that happened with my spouse's death was in the physical sense. I believe I still have and hold her, love and cherish her. She is in my heart, my soul, my everyday routine. And although *it's not the same*, I can make the best of what it is now through memories. Memories can make us feel like we belong somewhere, that we exist, that we are alive.

As I live my new life without my wife, I hope to be empowered by loving memories.

New Year, New Beginnings,
Old Feelings, Fond Memories

Happy New Year 2009! Do you remember when the big deal was the *year 2000*?

Time moves so quickly as we all get older. The seasons seem to change faster. Our lives can become more complex and emotional as we continue with our grieving process as the year advances to a fresh new number.

So much of our lives are based on *time*—time to learn, to be educated, to grow, to understand, to encourage, to be liked, to love, to be in a relationship, to marry, to have children, to own a home, to celebrate, to be in sadness, to grieve.

We often say that "there isn't enough time" or "when I have time, I will…" or "there is no time." We talk about time and we experience time, and hopefully, we are able to spend the right amount of time doing the things we love to do. We also hope that we are able to spend the most amount of our time with those we love.

Time is something that when lost, not given, or taken away from you cannot return to you. Time matters, and what you do with it is even more important.

As a new year begins, people like to reflect on time past and look forward to time in the future. Those of us that grieve the loss of a loved one look at time a little differently. Time can be a burden to us. Perhaps there is too much time to think about there being too much time when alone. We tend to look at the next twelve months as being another hurdle to get through with all of the special dates that use to be part of our lives when we were with our spouse. This will get easier, in time.

Our attitude and outlook should gradually develop to accept those things that we cannot change. Sound familiar? We have to be able to have the desire to move on, even if it is in a little sort of way. Moving on is difficult for many of us. Some of us are living in the past yet, relishing those wonderful moments we shared with our husband or wife. There is nothing wrong with that, and you can always remember those fond memories and old feelings. No one can take that away from you. You cannot be satisfied with that though. You must develop the courage to move forward, and when that mood strikes you, you will take a step in the right direction, a step that may take you to a place in your life that you can have those fond memories and old feelings as well as the new beginnings of a new year and new life.

What can we do to become closer to the old self we once knew we were? What activities did we stop doing or places we stopped going to? Who is in our circle of friends? Who isn't? What can we do to change that? Is here something we always wanted to try but never did, a place we wanted to visit but never went? Maybe this is the time to think of moving closer to these kind of opportunities to reach out, discover, and be part of a new experience in our life.

I know this is easier said than done. But we all must try to become better at this, myself included. Taking the chance, the opportunity, the courage to take a small step toward a small recovery of ourselves in the New Year will help promote and foster a small sample of a new beginning for our lives. In the end, wherever that is, we will become stronger and better at who we are. Let's face it, we are new people now without our spouse. We are different, we are changeable and we need to recognize this in order for us to be more comfortable with who we are to become in this New Year and in our life.

The Change of the Season

Welcome spring!

As the first day of spring came, I am reminded of all the "firsts" we experience in our lives.

Our entire life is built upon firsts. From infancy, we celebrate firsts in our lives and the lives of our family and friends—first steps, first birthday, first tooth, first day of school, graduation, first car, first job, marriage, first child, first house, first grandchild, and it goes on and on.

We celebrate firsts with those that we love. We share firsts with those that we love. We build a life of firsts with those that we love.

As the firsts happen, and we continue with our lives, it's taken for granted and becomes part of our lives that all of these kinds of things will happen with a companion, a partner, a wife, or husband. That is the beauty of life itself, that we are able to share events and happenings with those that we love, and the sharing is what makes it all so special.

When we lose someone very close to us, the firsts of life as they continue without our loved one are looked upon differently. It becomes difficult to be part of a first-time event or situation alone. You may have friends and family with you during these firsts, but it is not the same without your partner. You feel it, and it makes you very sad. At times, this can become overwhelming to you that you put off these firsts because you just can't do it yet. That's okay. You will know when you are ready to tackle the challenge of dealing with something for the first time without your loved one.

Being ready will not mean that it will be easy. The first time you go to an appointment alone may even be difficult and something that you avoid for a while. The first time you go grocery shopping alone or to a movie alone may be difficult. The first time you come home to an empty house will have its own impact on you. The first time you are out with others and there are more couples than those that are there alone will bother you.

The calendar year will play its role with you as well. All of those first holidays, birthdays, and anniversaries without your loved one will be a struggle for you because you are used to sharing those moments with them. Sometimes, the second, third, and fourth years may be difficult too. The day of the week and the date of their passing may affect you.

These are struggles that we have in common, struggles that are unknown by those that aren't experiencing this. You will eventually be able to handle all of these, some easier than others, but you will handle them. There are some things I have yet to do, go through, let go, become, visit, and talk about. But these things, in my own time frame, will be completed someday.

The *change of the season* provides us with a new outlook, especially springtime—new growth, new birth, new beginnings. It is up to us to either dwell on another season as it changes and stay trapped in negative thoughts and feelings or to embrace it, be positive, and make it the best that we can as we move forward one season at a time.

Does Anybody Really Know How We Feel?

As I continue with my life without my wife, I see changes in my world.

My world has been so very different since her passing. Some of the traditions I am still trying to hold onto, while others have been stopped or soon will be stopped. It's hard to hold onto something that only mattered when there were two of you that enjoyed it. When there is one of you left, the fun goes away. Each year is different in its purpose to me. The purpose is for me trying to understand and accept life that is so different than the many years I have spent with my wife.

These kinds of changes have to be looked upon as a positive in your life. You must recognize that you are ready to let go of some of the things while trying to build upon new things that matter to you. In your own way, at your own pace, you will find new things. It will never be the same as it once was, but it can be new to you, and it can become part of your new life without your loved one.

Some of us that go through this grieving process view the outside world differently now.

There are times I don't want to have any part of it, and on weekends, I just want to stay indoors and watch it move on through my window. I am content with that, and that alone time allows me to reflect in my own private world of my house. I reflect through thoughts that are translated by pen and communicate to others only if I wish to. Other times, I feel like I need to be around people, even people I don't even know. I want to be part of their world and be in places they are in like parks, malls, restaurants, or events. Being around others at times supplies its own sense of belonging to me when I want to be a part of the outside world.

The people around us really don't know how we feel. Those that are neighbors, friends, coworkers, even family members just don't get it. They think that our grieving process can be compared to a bad cold or sore back, and in a few weeks, we will be good again.

They can't understand our confusion, tears, sensitivity and, sometimes, our unwillingness to be part of their day. They question our emotional state and suggest that there must be something wrong with us that it is taking so long to get over it. "It"—imagine someone referring to us being robbed of our loved one way too early as an "It"?

There are people who really do know how we feel. Where do you find them? A bereavement support group. I am a firm believer in support groups, any kind of support groups that are existing to help those that are in need to become better at who they are or help to cope with a situation in their life like the loss of a loved one. Being part of a bereavement support group will allow you to express yourself to others and listen to others. This is such a great healing process because it provides you a sense of not being alone in your grief. Continued attendance in support groups builds a bridge that will allow you to slowly cross to the sunny side on your journey through this process. Being part of multiple bereavement support groups has helped me and continues to help me cope and stay focused with who I am and where I am going with my life.

If you are not part of one, I encourage you to do so. You have nothing to lose but some pain and heartache that you are feeling, and you will not be alone in your grief.

Reflections on an Anniversary

One's wedding anniversary after your spouse has died can be so heartfelt and sad. This past June was my fourth one without her, and it continues to be difficult for me. As time moves on, sometimes the recognition of this kind of event can be laborious. This would have been our thirtieth wedding anniversary, and a trip to Hawaii was going to be our celebration.

On June 23, 1979, we said "I do" and began a wonderful companionship and marriage that had the potential to last more than the twenty-six and a half years we had together. I met Sue four years prior to our wedding, and we became friends first as we fell in love and realized that destiny was to bring us together as a couple.

Sometimes you don't realize what you are missing until you no longer have it. This can apply to a marriage, a partnership, a loving bond between two people that share their lives together. I miss the recognition of our wedding anniversary, the celebration of another year of wedded bliss with the one I was meant to be with, the one that provided me with the love and support I needed over the years, the one that I loved spending time with shopping, going on vacation, taking walks, drinking specialty tea, riding bikes, going to the theater, eating dark chocolate, watching a movie, going out to dinner, or just staying home and being together.

So on our anniversary this year, it was me alone. With the fondest of memories, I made a toast to my wife with a glass of wine at the end of the day. I am thankful for the time I did have with her and the memories that I will treasure forever.

"The person who has memories is never alone."

My Eyes Are Open, but No One Is Home

I still have my bad days, those days that it takes all I have within me to get through the day functioning seminormally to those around me, those days that you just can't stop thinking of the loved one you lost way before their time and why it happened to them and to you.

It doesn't matter how long ago it happened, we all have bad days. We have those days that only we can identify with, days that our eyes are open, but no one is home. We are going through the motions of living for the day, surviving the time of the day at home, at work, or with our family and friends. And although they think we are doing fine and we are with them and part of the functioning of the day's events, our mind is somewhere else, somewhere in the distant past with our memories of our loved one and wonderful times past.

We relive our last time together, the last day, the last moments. We wish we could have had more time regardless of the circumstances, and we cry. We cry inside and to ourselves, but to those around us, we appear okay and doing fine. It's very difficult to go through a day like this for us, but we do it, we make it, and we hope that the next day isn't one of those bad days for us. We hope and pray that theses bad days come few and far between for us. We don't like experiencing them and hiding them from those that don't understand us and what we are going through.

We begin to understand that these bad days we experience are part of our healing process. We actually begin to respect that we have them and accept those days as being okay for us to go through. We allow ourselves to experience them without getting angry about it and try to not allow our personal inside feelings to affect the people around us. This is how we function during these bad days with our eyes open to the outside world, but in reality, no one is home inside to reflect us being all together with the present reality.

So we put on that "mask" to those around us, and everything appears fine to them while we are hurting inside from the thoughts and reflections that we are experiencing. The day will pass, and we will become better with time. And these bad days when "no one is home" will slowly decrease in frequency, and we will become whole again and at peace with ourselves.

The Still of the House

I miss the human side of how the morning comes and the day begins. The house is so still without her.

No more touch on the shoulder or voice saying "I love you," "Good morning," or "how did you sleep?" There is no more two-way conversation that fills the house. I miss that. I still speak to her at times, but the silence of the house is evident.

Through the shades and the curtains, nature provides the bright sun or raindrops on the window to announce the day and awaken me.

Usually, the first sound heard in the morning are the birds singing outside my window, or sometimes, it is the lone mourning dove on the window ledge with his early greeting.

I am dwarfed by a queen-size bed that at one time was too small on some nights for both of us. How I long to experience being crowded one more time.

The hearty bark of Hal, my dog, greets me as my feet hit the floor of my bedroom which is above where he sleeps in the family room. I am so thankful for Hal and all that he has meant to me as the only other boarder in the house.

The only voices I hear are those from the electronic medium of our world—TV, radio, and those that are from songs we enjoyed together or those that I now enjoy alone that make me think of her.

The only footsteps heard are my own. The only lights that are on are for me. The dishwasher runs less, trash is hardly anything, and the washing machine whirls fewer times these days.

The kitchen is still. Nothing is stirring, not even a wooden spoon in a mixing bowl, for her talents in cooking and baking are no more, and dust settles on pots and pans that were once brimming with delicious recipes and baked goods.

I miss the scents of home-cooked meals, the smell of her hair, and the perfume of her choice.

I miss the sounds of her presence—the running of the sewing or embroidery machine, the whistling tea kettle, her calling the dog, her voice on the phone, her playful laugh,

The lack of it all contributes to the stillness I experience.

Even though I experience the "still of the house," I am able to appreciate the memories that made it, at one time, full of life. I will always have love within my heart and soul for my wife. When I fell in love with her, it was forever.

We Miss Our Friend

Our friend loved us, and we loved them.
Our friend was kind, considerate, and compassionate.
Our friend respected us, admired us, and was proud of us.
Our friend loved to talk about us.
Our friend was patient with us.
Our friend was always there when we needed them.
Our friend never hesitated to comfort us, be with us.
Our friend walked with us, touched us, and hugged us.
Our friend loved to shop and always shopped for us.
Our friend was a companion and someone we learned so much from.
Our friend spent time with us, laughed with us, enjoyed quiet times with us.
Our friend was friends with so many others and always considered others before themselves.

We shared a friend that we loved and who was special to each of us in totally different ways, and our friend loved all of us unconditionally.

Our friend was Sue, and she was taken away from us.
We were saddened by the loss of our friend but were fortunate and blessed to have spent time with her.

We are Dom, her husband; Mandy, her daughter; and Hal, her dog, And...

We Miss Our Friend.

Silence

Silence is part of our lives. There are many places where we have to be silent or allow minimal sound such as a library, a place of worship, a hospital, or a museum. Some people like it to be silent in their homes or in their cars while they drive.

We like the presence of silence after a full day with children or grandchildren or even a tough day at work. We look forward to silence at bedtime or when we are reading an interesting book. It seems much more silent after a fresh snow fall. Early in the morning when taking a walk, it is more silent to us with less traffic in our neighborhood or on a trail in a wooded setting.

Silence can also be deafening and not liked by some of us.

When we have lost a spouse, silence is very prominent in our lives. There are no more conversations with them, and just the lost sound of their voice is disturbing to us. We long to hear them talk again, even though there were many times in the past we wanted them to stop talking. Now we'd love to hear them just one more time.

Sometimes, not having someone else in the house or the apartment is too silent. The sound of silence with no movement by another person or knowing that no one else is with you where you live can be troubling. Silence dominates our lives where we no longer have anyone to share the daily mail with or the opinions we formed about the news of the day. We lack a partner to eat with, to go out with, and to nap with. In many respects, we have lost a social connection to the "outside." Social silence can be difficult to deal with.

We have a choice to "break the silence." We have the ability to make our lives become whole again in some small way. It will never be the way it was, but it can become better than how it is for you now.

One suggestion to break the silence can be music. Music can make you feel better about situations. I listen to many songs during the course of a day that make me smile, recall an event, a happy moment in my past, a feeling that I am thankful to have had my wife be part of my life. Watching a favorite movie that we shared together also helps me. Volunteering for a cause and helping others can be beneficial to break the silence while communicating with others in a role that will bring you a sense of peace.

Being part of a club or organization that has weekly or monthly meetings will allow less silence and more sharing of thoughts and ideas with others. Reaching out to family members and friends to have dinner with or attend an event with are also ways to "break the silence" for us.

Silence isn't always a bad thing for us. There is a place for it. I find silence comforting at times to reflect and write. Silence helps me clear my head of thoughts and concerns and allows me to let go of sadness through methods of meditation. There are times I look forward to a little silence to feel the presence of the love I still have for my wife.

You must be able to be the one in control of silence in your life. Whether you want it or not, it should be a choice, not a sentence. You must encourage yourself to *break* the silence when you *need* to or *cherish* the silence when you *want* to.

Freedom to Choose, Freedom to Move Forward

Freedom can mean many things to many people—independence, ease of movement, a right, liberty, the capacity to exercise choice, free will, exemption from unpleasant or onerous conditions. Freedom for the bereaved takes on another meaning although many of the above meanings can be a part of it.

We lost a loved one, one who meant the world to us in our daily lives, one who loved us for who we are, one who played a significant part in our world every moment of every day. We are devastated, depressed, sad, and feel trapped in another world, the world of grief.

It is very easy to stay in this world, but it is not healthy for anyone. We all will eventually reach a point that we will experience the need to make changes by our own recognition or will be forced to do something because it is time to do it. The changes I speak of could be minor in nature, but each change brings us closer to a small moment of recovery.

Changes that we make as we grieve are not wrong, nor are they a bad idea to be avoided. On the contrary, change is good. Each of us has our own personal timeline of bereaving. No two people are the same. The impact that the death of our loved one had on us is so dependent on many personal factors of each of our lives and the relationship we had with our loved one. That said, a calendar does not dictate when it will be over.

My wife passed about four years ago, and it has only been recently that I started thinking of me and what I am going to do with my life now. After many years and moments of soul searching, I decided to make a decision that will change the direction of my life. My life is now my own. I do not share it with her, and I have me to take care of. My recent decision will set in motion future decisions that will continue to be made to move forward. That first step, that first choice was definitely the hardest for me, and I would think it to be the hardest for anyone. It's been a matter of a few months since that decision was made, and I have no regrets. I have had the time to search who I am and what I want to become, and I am okay with that. In a few more months, another choice will be made and then another and then another. Life continues, and I continue with it, trying to become whole once again as a person, as the new normal I am destined to become.

Making choices and moving on does not mean you are forgetting your loved one. In fact, I feel that you are taking them with you in your new adventure. They are in your heart forever, and the memories of the life that you have shared together will always be there to reflect upon. My wife's spirit lives within me, and I feel that she is guiding me on this journey of recovery from my grief as I move forward to accept the challenges that life has in store for me.

I Thought We Were Going to Grow Old Together

I wish I had a dollar for every time I heard this mentioned among those of us that grieve the loss of a spouse. We all believed that. And why shouldn't we? Life is grand for us in a relationship that is filled with love and companionship. No matter how much or how little amount of time we shared with one another, life was good.

Our partner is diagnosed with a terminal illness. They become very sick, very fast. They sustain an injury that becomes life threatening. Our soul mate has a heart attack, a stroke, an aneurysm. They have an accident at work or while they are enjoying a favorite sport or pastime. Our significant other is killed while on a boat or by a train or in a plane crash. They are killed in a vehicle accident or drown, or even murdered.

However it happens, they are gone. Life as we knew it is gone with them, for it will never be the way it was from now on. We were comfortable with our partner and our lives together. We did not see this coming. No one did.

There was so much more that we wanted to do together, share with one another—travel, explore new adventures, dine out more, visit friends and family more frequently, take extended weekends, and *grow old together*. None of that can happen with them anymore. We are shocked and somewhat traumatized by this life-changing event that, in some cases, happened in the blink of an eye, while in other cases, death lingered on for some time.

Regardless of the circumstances, we now begin another part of our life but not before we accept the reality of the grief that we feel and the emotional experience that won't go away. Our grief journey begins here. This journey is not one to take too lightly. It will be difficult at times, and you cannot do this alone. Support from family, friends, counselors, and bereavement support groups may be needed and are there for you to gain a sense of healing and balance within your life.

After months, maybe years, you will begin to feel better, and as time marches on, so will you. Our loss will eventually not dominate our thoughts, and we will have many past memories to reflect upon as we look forward to our future.

Although we are alone now minus our better half, their presence is with us, spiritually helping and guiding us through many tomorrows as we learn to live once again in a world full of hope and promise.

Reflection of Christmases Past

Where did this year go? Where did the last four years and eleven months go? That is how long it has been since my wife died in a vehicular accident three days after her forty-eighth birthday in the middle of January 2006. Sometimes it feels longer than that, much longer.

Christmas was *her* holiday. She was synonymous with Christmas. She made everyone around her feel the Christmas spirit, and she started talking about Christmas right after Halloween and planning it all to the day it arrived.

There are so many fond memories of our lives together during the thirty or so Christmases we spent together, beginning in our college days and continuing through our marriage. My memories of Christmases past include our daughter and her introduction to this joyous time of year as a child and watching her grow into the ideal of the Christmas spirit that should be in all of us.

My wife would wear a Christmas sweater each day in December leading up to *the day*, and she had enough of them to do that without repeating themes. She collected the North Pole series of Department 56 houses and would take such care and planning when setting them up around the holidays throughout the house. Trimming the tree, a real tree, was the big event for us.

The buildup toward the holiday is not there anymore for me. The sweaters are not worn but packed away, and the collectable houses are occasionally brought out and a select few may be displayed in her honor, but it's not the same. I still cry about her death. I miss her so much. The hole in my heart is getting smaller. It is mending a little each year. Life has changed for me and so many of us that have lost a loved one, and we feel it more around this time of year.

There is strength in the love and memories that we shared, and it's okay to go back there in time, but don't stay there. It is good to reflect, but acceptance to the new you and the new world around you is an important step. We have to look forward and move onward with our lives while still keeping our loved one in our heart and soul.

My Christmases will never be the same as they were with her, but I have created a different way of celebration of the holiday, and so can you. You must start new and accept that the new way is the now way. Your loved one's spirit will always be a part of you with each and every holiday you experience. My wife's spirit lives within me, and I reflect and am grateful of the time we shared together in Christmases past. Even though she is not with me physically, I know she is a part of everything I do and experience in life.

Lonely at the Fireplace

It had to be one of the best things we loved to share with one another, enjoy a nice fire in the fireplace in our home. We would spend the afternoon or evenings watching the flames dance on the seasoned oak logs, sprinkle some potpourri on the logs to bring out a beautiful scent or a treated pine cone to bring out bright colors. At times we would make popcorn, grilled cheese sandwiches, or even hot dogs over the fire. Toasting marshmallows was always an option as the fire died down and allowed us to create and enjoy a s'more or two.

I wanted to build a fire today in the fireplace, and I did. I wanted to make a connection with her. I needed to be close to her today, and this is the way I thought about how to do it. On the mantle are pictures of her and, around the room, some of her many cross stitch accomplishments that she took such pride in creating. Books adorn the bookshelves that were once read by her or acquired by her that she never got an opportunity to read. Trinkets and items are present that represent places we've been or times we had together. So many stories can be shared by looking at the various mementos—so many memories.

Sitting at the fireplace together was a highlight for us as a couple. We would share dreams, hopes, and plans for our future while listening to a favorite CD. Sometimes, we would sit silent in each other's arms, both content with each other's company just as it was.

So the fire continues to burn, and I sit here alone being part of a ritual once carried out by two people in love. I am glad I built a fire today and had some moments of reflection. I do feel that she is with me in a spiritual way, and even though it is *lonely at the fireplace*, I feel warmth in my heart from her.

Stop Asking Why

Those of us that have lost a loved one are familiar with the sudden unexplainable feelings of sadness and loneliness that we can feel in an instant, out of the blue, without any kind of warning or preparedness that it is about to happen. And it doesn't matter where we are or what we are doing, it is present and affecting us, and it is all so real.

These occurrences happen very often in the beginning of the grief journey, and with them happening so close to the loss, we could understand that it is happening and really don't question why. It continues throughout the first year, and as most of us can attest to, friends, coworkers, relatives, all say the same thing—"It takes a good year to get over it."

I am sure you shuddered at those words as I have. Most of those that never have been through a loss such as ours have no clue, and a year is not the marker that any of us should think that we will be healed like turning on a light switch. It's not that easy.

The second and third year comes, and these occurrences continue; however, they come less, and the duration of the sadness is shorter. During this time, we will start to question our own healing process and wonder if something is "wrong" with us. What we are experiencing is okay, and there is nothing wrong with us.

Time moves on, and we carry on in our lives, missing our loved one but realizing that we have to move forward in order to heal and get better with our lives. And then those feelings of sadness come again to us, and this time we are concerned and also question why. We will take time to analyze why. We may lose sleep over why. We may get sick over why. We will spend many hours, if not days, wondering why, but there are no answers to this question.

It still happens to me. It just did recently out of the blue, no warning, in an instant. I was spiraling down into sadness and loneliness right after having a pleasant evening at home watching a good movie. It came and went, and by the next morning, I was okay again.

I stopped asking why. There are no answers to these occurrences. I started accepting the fact that this will happen on occasion and that it is okay. It is part of the big picture of the grief journey that I am on. It does not come as often anymore, and it may eventually stop coming altogether. But I don't know, and I am not going to worry about it one way or the other. Acceptance should become part of your vocabulary. Be patient with yourself, and certainly, don't expect more than what you can handle at the present time.

What Can Help Me while I Grieve?

What can help me while I grieve? Talking with family and friends, finding something new to be part of, or crying. Speaking with your minister or priest and, perhaps, journaling. Reading about the grieving process in books, magazines, and online. Seeing a counselor or therapist, being patient with you. Allow time to heal your heart. All of the above can be helpful to you.

One other avenue to explore is *bereavement support groups*. Not enough good things can be said about them. I am a huge fan of these groups. They have helped me grow and still do to this day. I enrolled in my first bereavement support group about a month after my wife passed. It met weekly for six weeks. It was about ten people as confused as I was, all dealing with the same difficult issues that life has dropped on our doorstep. We were a collection of souls searching for an answer to a question: *Why me?*

Each time we met, we had an opportunity to be part of an experience that made us feel validated about our thoughts, feelings, and emotions. Words from others provided strength and knowledge in where we are and how to improve. Strangers to each other, but a bond developed among us for the reason of our attendance. Only those that have walked in the same shoes can understand and relate to you during this journey. The message is loud and clear. You are not alone.

Once that was done, I did feel better but needed more. And if you are one that feels that same way, don't stop there. Look for another bereavement support group that you can be part of and contribute to. I found one that meets monthly and is ongoing. The group was very accepting of me, and I still try to attend this monthly gathering as my schedule permits. I've noticed that when I cannot attend, I am missing something within me.

Bereavement support groups teach us all about ourselves through the discussions and emotions of others. We see ourselves through each other's grief journeys. We can recognize where we have been and hear about where we have yet to be and want to be.

We receive hope and faith through the process of this kind of gathering, and it provides a necessary pick me up that at times we so desperately need. We can talk about our feelings in a nonjudgmental atmosphere and feel comfortable with each other in that what we say is confidential. We also feel safe in this kind of place because we can vent, cry, be sad, and know that others in that room are okay with that.

People, at their basic level, don't want to admit to needing help and feel that they are weak to need something or even weak to ask for help. With grieving, most things that we should do take time for us to initiate to do it. We lack ambition, courage, and spontaneity. We lack support to *get* support at times. Nothing compares or comes close to (one to one) or (one to group) interaction.

Sometimes, those of us with many friends and family members think it unnecessary to be part of one because of the extra people in our lives. We fail to realize that at times, it is easier to talk to strangers about deep feelings and emotions than it is to talk with family and friends.

Online groups and websites can be helpful. Reading and expressing yourself on provided internet bulletin boards can be healthy.

In your time of need, it is the only "group" that will help you and be there for you, and you will be glad that you belong to it.

You may stop going to it at one point, but your membership is forever, and you'll never forget those that were part of it and helped you.

> Our community is dotted with shared experiences that can heal only when validated by another who has been there and who can ease the pain by truly understanding it. (Kenneth Doka and Joyce Davidson, *Living with Grief*)

Breakfast for One

Sunday morning breakfasts were something to look forward to. Whether we went out for breakfast or stayed home, spending time with each other and having breakfast on this non-work day was a treat.

As much as I enjoyed going out like anyone else, there was nothing quite like having a Sunday morning breakfast at home with my wife. It could be pancakes and bacon or Belgian waffles and sometimes, for fun, we had Mickey Mouse waffles made from a waffle iron obtained at a yard sale. They were extra good with powdered sugar and syrup.

I miss those Sunday mornings, mornings with a purpose and drive and a special time to share with one another.

I don't go out for breakfast anymore, not alone. I usually do have something special at home on a Sunday morning, but the place setting is for one. And as I enjoy breakfast, I think of all of those Sundays past when it was the two of us, and I smile at those wonderful memories.

Sixty Seconds More

All I want is sixty seconds more, sixty seconds to tell her how much I love her and miss her and to hold her and hug her. I want to walk with her and talk to her. I want to hear her voice just one more time. I want to look into her blue eyes. I want to hear her laugh and see her smile. I want to touch her hair and feel her breath.

One more day would be great, but I would settle for sixty seconds. A lot can be done in that time. Enough to allow me some closure and to say that goodbye I never had a chance to do. I would be satisfied with that and accepting with it, knowing that she has to go back.

Her death was sudden and unexpected. No chance to have that "sixty seconds more." No preparation, no advance warning, just shock and the trauma associated with seeing her car pushed into a building by a tractor trailer that was speeding and ran a red light. She never made it to work or home that evening. Her life ended as did some of mine.

I think of her all the time and hope that she is at peace in a beautiful place. I think of what more I would want to say to her and how best I can spend that sixty seconds with her. I know her spirit lives within me, and at times, I feel her presence guiding me and watching over me. I am very comforted with that. She was truly the best thing that ever happened to me, and I am so fortunate to have known her, fallen in love with her, and married her.

Our last words together were that morning when I left for work, and she was getting ready to walk the dog. None of us really know that those last words we speak to one another may be the "last" words. I didn't.

Each day is a gift. Respect it. Love it. Cherish it with your family and friends.

Entries from My Journal

Sometimes I have feelings as fresh as the day my wife passed, feelings of sadness, depression, despair, loneliness. I get chills. I cry. I wish I wasn't here alone without her. I know I can always dream, but I also know I can never have her with me again. I hope and pray I will be with her again in the afterlife.

I think I realized the separation between your heart and your mind. As much as your mind knows you have to be better, survive your loss—your tragedy—your heart has a different take on it. Your heart is with your soul and what you believe in, what you long for, what you miss the most.

It feels like it's been a lot more time than the four years since that day she was taken away from me. Time moving on without her is like a marathon of sadness. I hope and pray for a better day and the strength to endure, the power to heal, and the wisdom to learn.

Life around me looks different. People are different. I look at them through some kind of filter. Hard to explain but they (all people) appear different to me than before—before I came to be one and no longer part of a couple. So much is faith with all that we do and all that we are.

I want my old world back with you, Sue. You made things so easy to manage and were always thinking of fun things to do, and I loved your never-ending enthusiasm to make our lives better together.

I feel an incredible sense of presence with me today. Can't really explain it, but it was a warmth that made me feel good about life and how I am handling it without my loved one.

I feel alone at times early in the morning when I awaken for it is only me in this bedroom to greet the day and no casual conversation with anyone as the day begins.

Procrastination is the excuse I use for the fear of beginning new things in my life, but I eventually do them...but not without anxiety which I have trouble defining and understanding.

The hardest thing to accept is that your old life is gone and not coming back...ever. It takes years to come to terms with that, and even when you do, it's still tough to accept it.

I look at her picture and think it was light-years ago that we were one. I never thought that time would come and go, and only one of us would be present for its recognition.

Music is such a reminder of times with my wife. And although nice memories are a result of it, I'm also reminded of her departure from me.

Sometimes I feel like I step outside of my life without a memory of what I had for the past thirty years, like my past existence with her was in another dimension of time.

Death is so near to us—all of us. Every moment, every day. How many people are feeling what I am feeling right now? How many men? How many men lost their wife on the same day that I did and how did they die?

I feel so alone. I feel sad when doing simple things and to not have her here with me. Watching a sunset will never be the same without her sharing it with me.

The absence of a loved one that was taken for granted is very painful. We all are guilty of this, only to realize it more when they are no longer with us.

People forget what happened to me because I look *okay* and appear good to them. On the outside, yes. On the inside, I am hurting and continue to hurt all the time.

I continue to have difficulty coming home to an empty house from wherever I am at any given time.

Does life and death contribute to our destiny, our lives, our decisions, our wants? Will we ever know what causes life to happen or not happen?

It really comes down to the memories that keep you going, the memories of a beautiful life together, all the things we shared, talked about and went to.

The loss of a loved one makes you miss the potential—the potential of life experiences you will miss with them in the future.

II

Firsts

So much has been written and discussed in the bereavement world about "firsts." Emphasis is placed on that "first year," and then it is said that things "get better." There is no question that along with the terrifying first month or two, that the entire first year is an adjustment to a different life than the one you have had. For me, it didn't end there.

The second year was more difficult for me. I believe the shock I was going through the first year carried me along the way, going through the motions of life—waking up, eating, sleeping, repeat. It was this second year for me when reality set in, and I realized that what I have been through was not a bad dream but really did happen, and my loved one was not coming home again.

Any first event without your loved one, no matter how menial, can be difficult for you, and sometimes, even the second time or third time around of the repeated event is still unsettling to you.

My first birthday without her was difficult. I was turning forty-nine alone, and that was only four months after she died three days after becoming forty-eight. Anniversaries were another event that was tough to bear. My wife was a planner, and she had tentatively planned on major trips for us to enjoy about five years out, so whether it was one of our birthdays or an anniversary, we had plans of where to go and what to do.

One trip that was already booked and we were anxious to go on was to Belgium and Amsterdam, but that never came to be with her death happening three weeks prior. So for about five years after her death, there were those reminders that we were planning on an Italy trip, Alaska, or Hawaii, marking an event in our lives together. It was a relief, in a way, after I passed the five-year mark that there were no more plans to be reminded of.

There were many things that I experienced on the anniversary of her death (date of death day). The fact that it was three days after her birthday made it more difficult, but when it happened, it was on a Monday, and it was also Martin Luther King Jr. Day. I despised Mondays, every Monday, because weekly, it was a reminder that was the day of the week she died. Every year on Martin Luther King Jr. Day, there was the reminder as well as the date that it happened, the sixteenth. Probably the most difficult situation to deal with was when the sixteenth fell on a Monday again in the same month as her death. I was pleased that this didn't happen too often. I actually counted weeks in the beginning and could tell you what week number I was in since her death. This went on for the first year and a half, then I stopped doing that. It is amazing how we cope with difficult things in our life at times.

Change of seasons always present a challenge to most of us. If you and your loved one shared a favorite season, when it is time for that to roll around, it can be difficult. Sometimes, it is tough to go through a particular season alone, or maybe every season changing can bring some tears to your eyes. As with other observations that we are keenly aware of, seeing other couples walking together in the spring or the fall can make any of us feel isolated, not to mention all of the activities and events and holidays that are represented in just about any season.

Sue and I liked the fall and winter. We met during the fall and fell in love right after that in the winter, although Sue would say she fell in love and knew I was the one right from the start.

The fall and winter were happy seasons that we did much together, and most times, what we shared was simple and free—walks among the fallen leaves, going to pumpkin festivals, Halloween and Thanksgiving, building a snowman, sledding, catching snowflakes on our tongues, and Christmas. Of course, these favorite seasons of ours became extra special when we had our daughter to share them with too.

There was a set of serving trays that my wife liked by Currier and Ives. There were four of them, each representing a season. I wanted to buy them for us, but she insisted on only two of them, fall and winter. I still have them.

Firsts are usually recognized when we have to do things alone for the first time, and for me, it really didn't stop after the first year. In my opinion, there will always be a "first" coming up in your future without them. Some of us never notice them after the first few years, and that's okay. And you are in a better place than some of us. For me, I guess I am too open to the thought and the event and recognize a first many years later. I am not saddened by the recognition of the "first" I am going through at the moment. I merely recognize it and move forward. But I know it is there.

Some of my personal firsts besides the birthdays, anniversaries, holidays, seasons, changing records on everything by dropping her name, completing forms and no longer checking married, grocery shopping, banking, going to the mall, eating out which for me became taking out, seeing a movie, selling a house, buying a house, buying a car, opening a business, closing a business, retiring alone, teaching, continually responding (sometimes awkwardly) to those questions about "your story" to new people that you meet.

Everything and anything that you do (without them) now that you are a widower or widow is a first. And if you are feeling anxious and sad and troubled by it, it is okay, and that is why you are feeling this.

The firsts never stop coming. Things change in our lives. Friends come and go. Our own situations change, from careers to where we live to what we now believe in or feel comfortable with. Whether or not they are recognized by you, they are still there. Eventually, I will stop recognizing my own someday, and on that day, I will feel more at peace.

Change—Phase I

As anyone who has lost a spouse can attest, death of an intimate changes everything.

The freedom you once felt as being the person you are *and* the person you are with your spouse suddenly disappears from your world. You feel constricted, lost, and no longer in control of your destiny. You have been tossed into an environment that does not meet your needs of satisfaction, and you don't know what to do. And there is no one here to guide you along the way. In a sense, you lost your freedom.

So you slowly crawl back to some sense of normalcy, whatever that means. For some, it is the return to work and, with that, brings its own adjustments for you and those that work around you. For others, it is continuing on in a silent home or apartment, being alone for the first time from many years of married companionship. Whatever the return, you lost your freedom because you now feel compelled to continue on in the same manner that you have always done but, this time, without your spouse. It brings on a new dimension to life, a dimension of loneliness and loss that no one wants to be in. You feel locked into this new life at times with no way out.

I felt all of this, and I considered myself very fortunate that I was able to change direction in my life at one point. That point came about three and a half years after my wife's death when I just felt that I needed a change. My thoughts on a change were not small in scale. I felt that if I needed to do something different, why not go big? I had the resources and the desire.

After approximately thirty years in my field, I decided to retire. My employer was shocked, and no one really saw my intentions coming, but it was something that I had to do. I could feel it in my soul. I took a year to really think about my life, then decided to reflect, regroup, and relocate to another state and to open a small business. For the first time, I was on my own. There was not the comfort of a loving and supportive spouse to be there with me, but in a way, I knew she was within my heart with my need to seek out a new adventure. I also believed that there was more I was seeking besides a new adventure, but I couldn't identify what it was at the time.

I jumped into this with both feet and knew that I was heading into territory that I never experienced before, but I needed to focus my efforts on something totally different than my past two comfort zones. I looked at my life with my wife as being the longest comfort zone I experienced thus far, in general, and then the newest comfort zone of being without her while still working at my job for the past three-something years. The latter comfort zone was one that just wasn't sitting right with me. I felt the desire to do more, be more, and to better understand who I now was without her. I needed reflection time and thought that a new house in a new state with new neighbors was what I needed to do.

And so it began. I relocated to another state and began a small business in a town I never lived before and knowing no one. I should point out that my daughter lived about two hours from me in a neighboring state, so I did have family nearby that helped stabilize my new surroundings. The town was one that I had passed through before with my wife on our way to visit our daughter when she was in college and one that we also did the touristy things that couples do together, so it was not that foreign to me; I have been there before. There was a charm about it.

It was an experience that brought me closer to who I now was, and in many ways, it provided a necessary focus for what lay ahead of me. I met many new faces in a crowd of unknowns and also learned so much about life "out of the box" of my past comfort zones. I lived there for about three years, the last year with the business no longer a brick and mortar but an online business. Sales were not meeting expenses, and it was a necessity to close the physical business. No regrets. It was time. As it was time for me to move again. As I said before, this was something I had to do. I could feel it within my soul.

This was just a stepping stone. One of many baby steps on the journey I was taking trying to understand the new me and where I fit in. It was a necessary step and one that was needed to be completed to allow me to the next level of my being. Call it spiritual, intuition, gut feeling, but since my wife died, I have been guided by an unseen, unexplained light of some kind, directing my decisions and placing me among people and places I need to be introduced to and to experience their presence and share mine with them.

This experience that took me away for three years was also instrumental in allowing me to forgive. Since the accident that took my wife away from me, I was harboring actual hatred toward the driver of that tractor trailer. I realized that I was stuck in the past with this tragedy and could not get a grip on the life that I still had in front of me. Not forgiving was making me someone I did not want to be around, but the act of forgiveness is difficult to achieve. It was not happening for me while I lived in Pennsylvania around the same environment that connected me to all things familiar that kept me reminded of all that I lost.

Within six to nine months of living in a new state with a new house, new friends, and a new focus, I found myself meditating and praying for a new approach to my life. I realized that in order for me to move forward, I had to reach deep down within my soul and forgive the driver that took my wife away from me. I actually started thinking of him in a whole new light, wondering how he was coping with his actions of accidentally taking another life. Was he at the same job? Was he seeking therapy? How was he doing? This process provided me the opportunity to forgive, and it felt like a huge weight was lifted off of me. Forgiveness allowed me to live again without the burden of the past holding me back.

On the pages that follow will be reflections that I wrote to share with others through my newsletter and other newsletters since my wife died. There will also be a selection of entries from my personal journal that will follow the reflections. Most of the reflections and entries have appeared in the quarterly newsletter of *sudSSpirit*.

Reflections

Anniversary for Two Is Now for One

Another year has gone by, another wedding anniversary to mark without her. This past year was the sixth one without her. It feels almost like the first one without her which was six months after her death, very raw emotion, unsettled, pondering my future, and feeling like a lost ship at sea.

It does make you sad that you are the only one left to celebrate or recognize the day that once was and is no longer there. And many people can remember and think of you on that day, and that in itself is special and kind, but the one person that matters is no longer around.

It would always bother me when people would say that today is so and so's birthday, and they "would" have been sixty, indicating that they died or this "would" have been my fifteenth anniversary had my husband not died so suddenly. I often thought, why do that to yourself and bring back something that you feel bad about, stir up some old feelings that put you down and out?

I understand it now. I did it. I said to myself, this would have been my thirty-third wedding anniversary. And my recalling it in that way was to recognize and honor the day we became one as a couple, a memory of the times we had together as a couple for all those years and how strong our relationship was and how much we loved each other.

Our marriage was forever, but forever ended one January day in 2006.

I have known her for thirty years, married for twenty-six and a half years. Many couples had more time together than that, but many more had less. I am grateful for the time I did have with her. She was one in a million to me. As I move forward with my life, I will recall memories of our life together; memories that will bring a smile to my face, warmth to my heart, and a reflection in my soul. She is with me every day, and I will never be without her spirit in my heart.

Some Feelings Linger, but There Is Hope

My wife died on a random *Monday* in a winter month as a result of being at the wrong intersection at the wrong time. The driver of the tractor trailer was speeding and did not stop for a red light. She died instantly. She was on her way to work. She never arrived. She also never came home…alive.

I had the misfortune of discovering this while I was out tracing her route to work after receiving a phone call from her employer that she did not report to work that afternoon.

I look back at that time and wish I would have just gotten the terrible phone call that it happened or a call to report to the hospital or a friend/family member telling me in person. Anything would have been better, if there is a better, to be told this kind of news than to come upon the accident scene yourself.

That day haunts me and will probably haunt me forever. Every time I encounter that familiar scene of an accident like I saw the day my wife died, chills run through my spine, anxiety levels increase, and I experience a panic attack as I recall the past and how my life was changed in an instant. I was happily married eight thirty that morning, a widower that afternoon.

On a recent *Monday*, I encountered that familiar scene. I was on my way to an appointment when I saw a fire policeman blocking the road and detouring traffic. As I was led with other cars to take another road around the scene, I saw in the distance the grim tale of a vehicle accident with all the trimmings—fire trucks, ambulances, flashing lights, firemen in full gear, police cars, caution tape, and orange cones. It became all too real for me. I cried. I prayed for the people involved and their loved ones, and I prayed that all were *okay*.

On my way back on the same road approximately four hours later, the road was still closed, and once again, I was detoured with other traffic. It was then I had the realization that there probably was a fatality at this horrific scene, and someone somewhere was hearing this terrible news about their father, mother, son, daughter, sister, brother, aunt, uncle, husband, wife. What made this encounter more troubling and heartfelt was the fact that it occurred on a *Monday* while I was in the same car as I was when I encountered my wife's accident scene. *Mondays* will never be the same for me. Some feelings linger.

Later in the day, I heard on the news that there were two fatalities and two survivors from that accident. Life changed in an instant once again for some people, and they now have to struggle with their own life while dealing with the absence of the life that was lost.

This long journey ahead of them is one I can identify with; I am still on it myself. And it is through that journey that we discover who we are and what we are capable of becoming as a new person without our loved one. It will be frightening at times and sad, but through our memories of times past and our courageous efforts to move forward with our lives, things will fall into place.

Have faith and hope that you will become better. You will find a certain kind of calmness and peace that will allow you to breathe again and feel comfortable with who you are and the person you will become. Allow yourself the time that is necessary to heal. We all have different times and needs concerning this bereavement process. No two people are alike.

Attend a bereavement support group and participate with your heart. Allow your emotions and feelings to be shared with others. Listen to the others in attendance. Their thoughts will sound familiar to you, and you will feel validated.

Support groups are valuable tools that help you cope with feelings and emotions. Some feelings will linger, but they will diminish slowly with time and hope.

A *Walk in the Park*

I walk my dog every Sunday morning at a local park. He needs it as much as I do, and we enjoy that time together. Most times we are alone as we take this long walk, but occasionally, there will be someone else jogging by or walking alone too.

Today, there was a couple walking in the park hand in hand, and it hit me. When I actually saw this couple, I *saw* myself with my wife walking hand in hand as we have done so many times in the past in so many locations. I paused, and for a moment, I was *there* in the past with her and remembering the touch and warmth of her hand in mine.

We loved to take walks together. It started on a college campus and continued throughout our lives together—walks around the neighborhood we lived in at the time, walks around a local park or trail, walks around a city or country we were visiting at the time on vacation or an extended weekend getaway. Walking with each other was a way of connecting, talking, and enjoying each other's company. Walking together was fun and brought us closer together, sharing conversation and making decisions about our lives together.

It's interesting that there are times I see couples, and it does not affect me. And I am not sure why this time it did. Triggers like this happen, something that makes us remember our loved one or a past memory that we shared with them. Triggers are more prevalent in the beginning of one's grief journey, and as time allows, they become less frequent, but they can still happen to you. The difference is that you can handle them better and, in most cases, not be as bothered by them and continue on with your day.

It's okay to experience this. You lost someone you truly loved, and they have had a huge impact on your life. Embrace this. Accept it as another step on your journey toward a new you, a new beginning without losing your past experiences and memories with your loved one.

There is a new you out there now, and eventually, you will be able to accept it better and be able to deal with it even if it is only one step, one day at a time as you continue on your walk through your life.

Snow Falls, Memories Resurface

Fresh fallen snow, white and silent as it accumulates outside my window.

She made me look at snow in a whole new different way. We were in college, and it snowed. She decided to walk away from the shoveled path into the adventure of the drifts of snow that was around campus. I followed only to have the time of my life. We jumped through the snow, chased each other in the snow, made snow angels, threw snowballs at each other, made a snowman, and wrestled in the snow. When it was all said and done, I carried her in the snow. It was what she wanted all along. We laughed. We then headed indoors for warmth and some hot chocolate.

Those were the days...

We fell in love, got engaged, and then married, and our times in the snow continued.

We went sledding, continued to build snowmen, and the occasional snowball battle was not out of the question.

We loved to take walks in the snow while it was snowing to try to catch the snowflakes on our tongues and, on a moonlit night, even better, so silent and illuminated. A stroll in the snow during Christmas was extra special with all of the holiday lights aglow.

Watching the snow now brings back these wonderful memories. I treasure these memories. And as it snows, whenever it snows, I reflect on past times of our beginnings as well as our entire life together.

Snow and winter makes me remember. Perhaps the fall brings back memories for you, walks among the fallen leaves around a lake, or maybe the summer and time spent on a beach or on a vacation together. We all have triggers that allow us to remember happier times and are grateful that we experienced them with the one we love.

It was a great life I had with her, one that ended way too soon. Without her and her time with me, my life would not be as rich as it is today.

Missing My "Better Half"

We all know the phrase "where's your better half" as people refer to your partner, husband, or wife when they would see you without them on occasion or at events. The question meant a lot more than where is your partner.

Deep down, it reflected something that none of us realized. The "better half" played an important role in our lives as a couple, and we far too often took it for granted. I miss my better half. I believe my better half really was what the label implied.

She was the glue that kept things together in our lives. She was the planner, the organizer, the encourager, and the inspiration behind my successes. She made me feel comfortable about my life and living it to the fullest with her. She allowed me to grow and become things I never thought I'd be. She made me feel needed and wanted and never alone as I do now at times.

Those of us that have survived the death of our spouse knows that distinct feeling of aloneness that at times comes out of nowhere and overcomes us with great sadness. It is at those times when we know our better half is no longer with us to pick us up again. We miss them.

All of us at one time, or many times, have wished that the day it happened can be relived, and there would be something that we could do or something that could be done to prevent that tragedy from happening to them and to us. We wish that it was all a dream and we would soon wake up from a very long nightmare and life as we knew it would return.

It is not going to happen. We have to acknowledge this and understand that we probably can try to replace some of those feelings we experienced from our better half's involvement with another partner or a close friend or family member. We can also try to focus on ways that we can become a better person by ourselves through involvement with other activities that are rewarding to us and make us feel better.

Although my better half is no longer with me, she will always be within my heart and close to my soul, providing a comfort level that only she knew how to do.

The Story Behind the sudSSpirit Logo

I have been asked many times about the *sudSSpirit* logo, the cross with a peace dove and a flower at the base of the cross with the acronym sudSSpirit across the middle of the cross. The acronym stands for *s*udden *u*nexpected *d*eath of a *S*pouse *S*urvivors in *p*artici-pation to *i*nform, *r*enew, *i*mprove, and *t*riumph. The cross is another story.

I was never one for wearing any kind of chain or necklace, so when I received a silver chain with a sterling silver cross with a peace dove in the center of it one Christmas in the '70s, I wasn't sure how to react. It was nice and it was appreciated. And it was from my soon-to-be wife. I did wear it occasionally, but most times, it remained in the box it came in.

When I started traveling for work and went places that took me away from her for a few days or a week at a time, the necklace came with me, and I wore it to feel closer to my wife. And that worked for me. I started to become accustomed to it.

Wearing that necklace now *all the time* works for me. It is now a permanent part of my being and a way to always have the memory of her with me against my chest, close to my heart.

The gardenia flower was one of her favorites, and I bought one for her from a street vendor in San Francisco during a weekend get-away after taking a ride on a trolley car. We had a wonderful time in California, it being our first time there, and had the dream to return there again for another adventure, but that was not to be. I am so grateful that we took the time to travel there and many other places during our life together.

I miss my wife, and I know that she is around me in spirit, being proud that I took her passing and turned it into a positive to create a bereavement support group to help others cope with their grief journey.

A favorite flower plus a Christmas present from the distant past and an acronym became the reality of what represents *sudSSpirit* today.

Dogs Can Be a Griever's Friend

So much has been written about dogs and the role they play in our lives. Many people that I have known had a dog at one time in their life. Many more always had a dog and continue to have a dog that shares their life with them and their family.

Man's best friend, a child's playmate, a companion to you, their role and function to us is countless. And that role is one that is unconditional love and loyalty. They can't speak, but they know and realize all that is happening around them and, in their own ways, are able to provide comfort and a sense of peace to us when we need them to.

I had a dog growing up that was shared with my sister. After college and then marriage, a dog was destined to be part of my family. My wife always had a dog growing up and loved dogs as much as I did. When I look back at all the dogs we had in our home, they all played a significant role in that part of our lives that we were experiencing at the time.

Dogs were part of our marriage and the development of our family. Upon the arrival of our daughter, dogs continued to be part of our lives and hers. Children look at dogs so much differently than us adults, but they have their own place for them in their hearts.

Dogs love to be a part of whatever it is you are doing, whether you like that or not. They are loving, caring, and love to have your attention and be talked to. They seem to know when we are happy or sad and act accordingly to celebrate with us or help us.

There is a special dog in my life. This dog is one that my wife selected, and we became owners of a blue merle sheltie as a four-month-old puppy. My wife named him Hal. His birthday is on Halloween. Hal is adorable and very intelligent.

My wife and Hal became inseparable, and this dog did everything, went everywhere, and was always thought about in anything that was planned. My wife spent as much of her time with this dog as she could in many areas of adventure and experiences. Hal was put through many classes of instruction, being awarded with one completion certificate after another including therapy dog training.

Hal seemed to really excel in therapy dog training, and my wife loved to take him to visit those less fortunate in nursing homes and assisted-living facilities. Sometimes I wasn't sure who enjoyed bringing smiles to faces more, her or the dog. They were indeed a team in this venue and provided an extra dose of happiness to an otherwise drab day to the people in these elder care settings.

My wife's time with Hal was cut short when she died in a vehicle accident. She was only forty-eight; the dog was only three at the time. The hardest thing I ever had to deal with was the death of my wife; the second hardest was telling my daughter. The third was breaking the news to Hal. I remember walking into the house that day and being happily greeted by the dog as usual. I dropped to the floor and hugged Hal while sobbing for what seemed like hours. He waited at the kitchen door that night for her to come home. Hal seemed depressed and sad and wasn't eating and spent most of his time in a corner. He needed closure, and my daughter and I had a thought. We called the funeral home and took Hal there to see my wife, his master. I would not believe it if I didn't see it, but after seeing her lifeless body lying there, and no voice, movement, or touch was coming from her, Hal then realized that she wasn't coming home. It was a sight I shall never forget.

Dogs' emotions are no different than ours; he was saddened by the loss of his master and was in mourning for a while. We mourned together. We spent a lot of time next to each other. We cried and helped to provide comfort to one another.

Ironically, Hal became *my* therapy dog. I was now the one that he was helping with his charm and personality, his presence and kindness, his gentleness and kisses. He was helping me through the most difficult period of my life.

Life's challenges and changes can destroy us. Man's best friend has been there to help me and provide a comfort level that is indescribable. Hal has been a true friend and has helped me through my slow recovery from a life-altering situation.

Hal has helped me decide to retire from a thirty-year career and adjust to the new me that I didn't even know yet. He has helped me deal with my sadness and adjust to the loneliness over the years. Hal has helped me through all the "firsts" without her and the changing seasons with memories. And he is always up for *what's next* in our life together, just like my wife once was. Hal is always there supporting, encouraging, and loving unconditionally.

I am really not sure how I would have fared out in all of this "life" stuff had it not been for Hal. There has never been a dog like him before in my life, and I don't know if there ever will be again. He maintains a special place in my heart.

Hal is getting older, and signs of age are showing. I have to come to terms with the fact that he will leave me at one point to join his master who left both of us many years ago. When that day comes, another life-altering situation will happen to me. We must recognize that the sun sets and rises daily, time moves on, life continues. We move forward and take steps toward a better and brighter tomorrow.

I love my dog, Hal. He is responsible for helping me "make it" through my grief journey. I am grateful for his love, devotion, compassion, and presence in my life. Never underestimate the comfort of dogs.

Moonlight Feels Right

It was the night before the final day of July, and as I was closing the patio door for the night, I noticed the soft glow of light bouncing off the deck. I went outside onto the deck to discover a beautiful moon that was producing such moonlight.

My present world at the moment stopped while I took in this sight. I settled onto the chaise lounge and watched in awe of this spectacle before me. I seemed to be in some kind of trance, taken by the beauty that was in the cloudless sky. The stars were bright and plentiful this evening which added to the magic I was experiencing.

As I sat there admiring the sight, I heard sounds from around me—rattling dishware from a nearby neighbor, a phone ringing in the distance, a passing car on the street behind me, a few crickets chirping, and the sound of my own TV in the background coming from my open window.

I reflected about my life, where it has been, with whom, and how it came to be where it is today, at this very moment. Life is not perfect, and it is not easy. It is full of happy and sad times, mountains of success and valleys of stress, and there are no guarantees or sure bets about anything that is happening anywhere or anytime.

When it really comes down to it, *life* and how we live it is *all about attitude*.

How we react to life is what makes us who we are and how we come to be. We all have choices. We have the opportunity to determine what we want to be when something bad happens to us. Our reaction is dependent on our attitude and how we are going to handle things, accept things, learn from things. No one can do this for us. We must decide to do this on our own, and we must want to do this with conviction.

Charles Swindoll once said:

> Words can never adequately convey the incredible impact of our attitudes toward life… Attitude keeps me going or cripples my progress. It alone

fuels my fire or assaults my hope. When my attitudes are right, there is no barrier too high, no valley too deep, no dream too extreme, and no challenge too great for me... Life is 10 percent what happens to us and 90 percent how we respond to it.

Looking at the moon tonight made me think of all of this. The moon is like a beacon in the sky guiding us, helping us cope with our problems, dealing with the loss of a loved one, understanding our new normal, and trying to become a better person with a *new* attitude about our *new* life.

Noticing the moon tonight was a sign for me, a sign of encouragement, reflection, thinking of past memories and preparing for the next step on my journey into my future.

I actually thought of a song from the '70s called "Moonlight Feels Right" by Starbuck, one of many songs from that era that I enjoyed on a university campus with the woman that was to become my wife someday. These memories brought tears to my eyes about everything I was feeling at the moment.

My one wish tonight would be that my wife was with me, enjoying the moonlight as we have done many times as we took evening walks together.

As I was wishing on this bright moon tonight, I believe my wish came true because I felt her spirit in my heart. The moonlight sure does feel right.

Rediscovering the New You

Losing your spouse or significant other is painful, very painful. Any loss comes with much anxiety, sleeplessness, uncertainty, shock, trauma, and the realization that your world as you knew it ceases to exist. It is you, alone, and any reference to your better half or to you as being part of a couple is gone, long gone.

Friends and even family members look at you so much more differently than ever before. There is a sense of discomfort with you around. No one knows how to act or what to say around you, and it is okay. You didn't know how to act or what to say around those that you knew that lost someone close to them. Our society does not know how to deal with others who lost a loved one. It's not exactly something that is "gone over" in our development as people or in any education process. I believe we need to work on that.

All of the stages and phases of grief that have been talked about, written about, researched about are all clear and defined. We read about them, share them with others going through the same thing we are going through in support groups or in a one-on-one counseling session with a trained professional. And that is all good and under-stood, but sometimes, everyone's phase or stage isn't exactly like what they say or one goes through. That is okay. Realize that each one of us are going to go through this journey in our *own* way, on our *own* time schedule. Knowing this and accepting it will help you in many ways so that you don't feel like you are alone out there and isolated from others.

The benefit of support groups is that at times, those that are in attendance are at these different phases of their grief compared to you and to the others, and that can be very helpful. Listening and sharing among each other allows everyone to learn from each other and feel a little bit better about where they are on their journey. This is a healthy feeling when you realize that someday you may feel bet-ter than you do right at that moment because others who have been there have survived it, and they are there to prove it and talk about it.

It may take a long time, a substantial time, to rediscover who you now are. And at times this discovery happens in small increments over a period of time. So if you think once you discover something new about the new you and that's all, just wait because there will be something else that will be coming along at another time. This is a process that seems to not end as we think it might. At least, that is what I am experiencing. I am still discovering and finding out many things about myself as I make this journey.

I have been through and have put myself through many changes and challenges in my life without her, and all of it was worth it—the good, the bad, the indifferent, the successes as well as those things that just didn't work out the way I thought they would. But I tried and became a better person for trying and certainly have learned a lot about me along the way. You know what they say; when life gives you lemons, make lemonade. Turn a negative into a positive for yourself and others.

All of us that are going through this grief journey face challenges. We may not think of them as challenges and changes as they are happening, but afterward, we realize that we overcame it and got through it. Facing situations alone for the first time can be very difficult. Those "first times" don't all come within that first year either, contrary to what most people outside of our grief world believe or have read about from people who have *not* been through this, another point we have to become better at.

Firsts can be as simple as grocery shopping alone, and for one, to a more complicated and complex situation like moving out of your house that you shared for many years. The birthdays, date of death days, anniversaries, season changes, they all factor into rediscovering the new you. Changing careers, retiring, beginning a new job that you didn't have to have before but is now a necessity, they all factor into rediscovering the new you. Changing your diet, health concerns, new socialization circles, learning to do things you'd never thought you had to worry about, they all factor into rediscovering the new you.

And it is okay. You can do this. You have to believe in yourself and have faith and hope that better days are ahead, and they truly are for you. Stay confident, focused, and learn to accept the new person that you are becoming, a person that looks forward to new experiences, enjoying life, and laughing again.

Sunday Pasta

When I was growing up, Sunday was pasta day. It was rare if we did not have pasta on a Sunday. It was anticipated and delivered by my mom's great cooking. And it was an experience of enjoying food together as one.

When I was married, we had pasta on Sunday occasionally, and it brought back memories of my childhood and growing up in those early years. My wife and I would enjoy a meal together prepared by her with love.

I had pasta today, and it is a Sunday as I write this to share with you. I experienced a mix of emotions and feelings of my childhood with my family as well as my married life with my wife, Sue.

The pasta was great with a glass of wine and some toasted garlic bread, but something was missing. My family wasn't with me, nor was my wife. My dog was at my feet as I enjoyed my dinner, keeping me company as he has done these many years without her.

I enjoyed my dinner and reflected on how fortunate I was to have had such a wonderful family growing up that provided me with these kind of warm memories and how extra lucky I was to have met a girl at college and began a life together as a married couple, a life that was filled with joy, companionship, and shared interests that made us the best for each other during our time together.

Enjoying pasta on a Sunday is one of those things that I occasionally do and remember. It is only one of many memories that bridge the gap between the past and my present reality, and it feels good to acknowledge this and accept it.

I am sure there are many memories that you have that can help you bridge that same gap that exists in your present life. I encourage you to allow your fond memories to help you open up and experience the joy in remembering.

As long as you have memories, you are never *really* alone.

My Favorite Chair

It was an evening around sunset, and I just reentered the house after playing with my dog out in the backyard. I sat in my favorite chair that I recently had reupholstered. The chair is in my family room, and while sitting there at sunset, I was able to watch the sun slowly go down in between the branches of the trees in my backyard with my dog, Hal, at my feet. I enjoy the feeling of this chair, and now with its new look, it felt even better. Sitting on this chair has always provided me with comfort and peace.

Let me tell you about this chair.

My wife and I bought this chair on sale at a family-owned furniture store near our home at the time. We both liked the chair which was a Flexsteel brand known for its durability and oak frame. It was comfortable and well-made, and it seemed to fit you just right as you sat down into its soft embrace with firm arm supports.

Through the years, furniture was bought and sold, but this chair stayed part of the family, perhaps more so by my own desire to hold onto it, not sure how much attachment my wife had to it over the years. The dogs we owned also liked the chair to my dismay.

Throughout the years since my wife died, I have been through many life changes and challenges, some I instituted while others just happened. We all go through life's journey in different ways and experience the triumphs and tragedies. With my relocation, many things that were possessed did not make the cut to come with me, and some of the things that did come eventually found a new home elsewhere with someone else. My favorite chair remained, and I thought it would be time to give it a new look.

I found a local upholsterer who said that he could do it, and it would be less expensive if I found material he had in stock that I liked. I wanted to find a blue pattern for the chair, and his selection for blues was limited to one, but this blue pattern was a winner in my book. In fact, the only blue he had was the same kind of material that was currently on my chair. It was material used for Flexsteel furniture products, but instead of the tan pattern it now had, it was done in a blue and had a flower design that almost matched the current pattern. What are the odds of not only picking this upholsterer but also him having only one blue color that I liked and it being the same fabric used on this kind of chair from the manufacturer? I guess things happen for a reason. He did the chair in two days for a great price. My wife would be proud of me getting such a great deal.

I began to reflect about the chair as I sat in it as the sun was setting. Do I like the chair for its never-ending comfort, or as I now realize, do I like the chair because it is the last piece of upholstered furniture I own that I bought with my wife? Or is there something else that draws me to the significance of this chair?

The chair was purchased at that family-owned furniture store I mentioned earlier. The location of that furniture store is the same location of the intersection where my wife died in a fatal vehicular accident just over seven years ago. Inside that furniture store was where I learned of the life-changing news and collapsed in anguish to the floor in the midst of police and first responders.

Many years ago, I was standing in this store on a happy occasion purchasing a chair with my wife, and now I was in a heap of crumbled humanity, trying to make sense of an unexpected death of my soul mate. What are the odds of this store location being the common denominator of two events in my life (one happy, one tragic) separated by many years? I never thought about this chair in that regard until now. I guess things do happen for a reason.

Giving the chair a facelift allowed me to give my life new meaning, new direction, moving forward but retaining the comfort and peace of a life once past; a life that was shared by two that bought a chair together and now a chair enjoyed by one.

The chair is more than a piece of furniture. It tells a story and brings back some nice memories and, in an important way, connects to life's triumphs and tragedies and remains a meaningful presence in my new world.

I will always keep this chair. It was once a part of us and now is part of me. The chair symbolizes a safe place to be, to relax, to read, to nap, to meditate, and to watch a sunset on any evening anywhere I live.

Life Is Fragile

It seems that all of us are in a race everyday of our lives and are so caught up in the moment of trying to do more, be more, and get more that we forget about the most basic of virtues of being a good person to our fellow man.

We do not value life as much as our forefathers have. We do not even think about the chance that life can be over, finished, done in an instant. The near misses in life are all too frequent, and most of us move on from those misses without learning anything from them. Life as we know it can change in the blink of an eye, and if we don't use our time wisely with our loved ones, friends, and taking time for us, we will regret what we never did, never said, or where we never went.

If we would only realize the fragility of life for ourselves and those we love, we all would be so kind and appreciative of everyone we come in contact with. My outlook on this life of mine has changed since the death of my wife, and I do my best to realize that in any instant of time, it can all go away. I live for the moment, for the experience, for the enjoyment of what life can bring me and the love for those around me.

Treasure the time with your loved ones and friends. It's the little things in life that means the most to all of us.

I Miss Her Blue Eyes

My wife, Sue, was killed in a vehicular accident in January 2006 when a tractor trailer ran a red light and struck her vehicle broadside, ending her life instantly. Her forty-eighth birthday was three days prior to her death.

My wife, my soul mate, had many wonderful qualities and traits. She had the prettiest blue eyes, and I would love to look into her eyes and be in such awe at the beautiful person she was within. She always looked good in anything blue, and when she wore blue, her eyes were a natural accent. When I look at pictures of my wife, her blue eyes are so defined and prominent that you almost feel like she can talk to you. I bought a blue topaz necklace along with matching earrings for her birthday one time. She always looked stunning whenever she wore them.

As the last week of May approached a few years after her death, I had many reflections of our life together. We have known each other for about thirty years and were married for twenty-six and a half of those. I remembered that I proposed to my wife the last week of May, a year before we were married. The last week of May would also be the due date of our daughter four years later. Our daughter was two weeks late and was born in June, the same month as our wedding anniversary.

I cannot explain what had drawn me to a jewelry counter during the last week of May, but something did. In the case on display was a blue topaz men's ring. I was drawn to this and asked to see it. It was the only one they had, and it was in my size. Better yet, it was also on sale, something that my wife always looked for, a sale. I had to buy it.

I decided to wear it on June first, the beginning of a month, the month that celebrates our daughter's birthday and our wedding anniversary. Wearing this ring for the first time gave me a sense of empowerment. I felt confident, at peace, and in a way, I felt my wife's presence within me.

It was incredible how this ring made me feel. I am glad I bought this ring. I like to wear this ring occasionally, along with another ring that she purchased for me many years ago. When I look at and feel this blue topaz ring on my finger, I think of Sue and her beautiful blue eyes, and it makes me smile. It is all about remembering and reflecting and continuing to move forward with our lives.

The Next Best Thing to Them Being There

There are perhaps dozens, if not hundreds, of things that we miss about our spouses, so many things that were taken care of and just done without us even noticing or thanking them for doing it. Taking one for granted comes to mind, and it is very difficult for anyone to not take a loved one for granted. It is just the way it is, and we often are the ones (the survivors) that say after their death, "I should have not taken them for granted." This statement comes after the shock wears off and the realization comes of all the things that you now have to do, to become, and to decide alone.

Their physical presence is no longer among us, and we realize how much the comfort of them is missing. We miss the kisses, hugs, and that often misunderstood but pleasing touch on the shoulder that provides that sense of comfort and peace knowing that we are in this together.

So where does that leave us? We must think about the next best thing to them being there and experience these small measures of magic that provides us with a memory and makes us smile.

It could be as simple as looking at photos of them with you or them doing something that makes you smile or laugh. Maybe you are fortunate enough to have them on a video or even have their voice recorded so that you can experience their movement and sound again. Hugging a pillow as you lay in bed and remembering their laugh or the way they sneezed provides us with a memory as does the scent of their aftershave or favorite cologne.

Sometimes we never realize that they always used to say something (a favorite saying) until we no longer hear that something anymore and miss them saying it. Remembering that can bring a smile to ourselves, and sharing that with others can make us feel good about the memory and feel their presence—souvenirs from places you have been, favorite books you shared, music that brings back a memory of where you both were when that song or group was popular, perhaps a concert or a play that you both liked and enjoyed.

Furniture that you purchased together as well as times at the fireplace that were memorable can stir the memories that you shared. Taking a walk on a favorite trail or visiting the place that you first met brings it all together and places you in the moment for remembrance.

We all must learn to *live in the moment*, the present, and know that they are with us, guiding us, and believing in us. It will provide us with a confidence level that will make our days fulfilling, and we will be grateful for knowing and loving them. We will also realize how rich our life is because of them and their influences on our being.

Being open to this along with the memories will allow us to feel that ultimate feeling one gets which is...*the next best thing to them being there.*

A Cup of Tea

I felt like having a cup of tea this afternoon. Did you ever get that feeling for a need for a cup of tea? Perhaps to make you feel warm inside or to relax or to enjoy a cup and just be.

I enjoy tea. I love coffee more but do like a good cup of tea. Having tea now reminds me of having tea with my wife who was a tea lover big time. Sue loved tea and would enjoy a cup with a favorite cookie. She would look forward to her tea time.

I still have a small tea set that she bought and would display. We actually had tea with it once together when she first bought it, and to see her delight and enjoyment made me smile.

I can't share "tea time" with her anymore, but it is nearly impossible to brew a cup of tea now without thinking of her. So maybe feeling like having a cup of tea this afternoon was the desire to remember and to think of her in a special way.

A cup of tea is one of many ways that I think of her and that she is still a part of my life, memories of times past, reflections of a happy life together, and gratitude for having her be an important part of my life. She will always be my *"cup of tea."*

Stumbling on the Past Brings Warm Memories to the Present

They were just there, right there in front of me. I have seen them there many times over the years and never really thought about them or paused like I was doing right now. But now I did. I paused and stared at them. I am not really sure what I was thinking, but I stopped what I was doing to take in their sight and just froze in my tracks. I picked them all up, still in their original boxes from the times they were purchased.

That's how I am. I always seem to want to and actually do save original boxes of things, not big things but things that I feel are important to save because they are special, and these are special. At least, that is what I am thinking right now as I hold them in my hands. But I guess they have always been special throughout the many years we had them. We cherished them, loved them, and respected them. We honored what they represented and knew what was behind their meaning and existence.

I stumbled upon them while I was looking in a drawer for something else, and I knew they were there but never really thought about them until now, at this moment.

There were three small boxes. I opened all of them one at a time to look at the treasure before me, a treasure that was once worn by both of us. The first box contained the engagement ring that I worked two summer jobs to pay for back in the '70s. The second box had her wedding band that was custom-made with three diamonds that would match up to how the engagement ring was designed. This box also contained an eternity ring with five diamonds. I bought this for her on our twentieth anniversary. The third box was my wedding band. All of the pieces are in gold, and all appeared lifeless in their respective containers. Picking them up and really looking at them brought back such wonderful memories of a life that we were blessed to share with one another.

Details around how I proposed as well as our wedding day and the adventure of life that we were on together all came back to me.

It was a warm and comfortable feeling, full memories of a wonderful woman, wife, and mother.

Then I had the strangest desire to have them cleaned. It was something that had to be done and right now. Something that I would have considered silly years ago was now an objective. I took the rings into a local jeweler and had them cleaned. When I picked them up, they possessed a sparkle that I have never seen before after they were cleaned countless other times. I am not sure why they appeared that way to me, but they did. I had to do this. Get them cleaned. I had to go down that pathway of the past and bring that up again for me, and I am glad that I did. I felt at ease. I felt peace.

These rings are an important part of me, of us, still. I am not sure if they are something I will ever part with, at least, not for now. But life continues to move forward as do I.

Maybe there will be another time in the future when I will be looking for something, and I come across them again and then I guess we will see how I react to that. One never knows why we react and do things and feel things the way we do. We just do, and we have to accept and not question why.

Do what feels right on your journey, on your timeline and no one else's. This is your journey. This is your new life without them. Take hold of life with both hands and know that you are not alone, and you can do this. You are a survivor, and nothing can stop you.

Maybe my wife wanted me to savor the moment of the rediscovery of the rings we both loved to wear. Who knows? It made my day, and I am glad for it. Sometimes, we never know what may be around the corner for us to encounter on this journey of ours. We must maintain faith and hope for a brighter tomorrow.

Oh, Christmas Tree

There it stands, so tall and proud and decorated so festively in any home, the symbol of a time of love, family, friends, peace and, in some ways, a representation of faith, hope, and all good things in the world.

The Christmas season is a delicate one for those of us that have lost a loved one. Christmas is so rich with tradition and full of memories of the way things are done and celebrated. We act accordingly to what we are known for doing during that season, and we very rarely stray from the tradition of what we always do.

So when something tragic occurs to us and things are now very different, then the holiday season comes around, we are placed in a position that is not very familiar to us. What we once had is no longer possible because a crucial part of the traditional plan and celebration is missing—our loved one.

What to do?

There is no right answer to this. You have to be guided by you and your feelings. There are countless articles, guides, suggestions out there for you to review and help you decide what is best for you. Please read them and keep an open mind for your situation.

What about the tree? What do you do with that thought?

This is where a dilemma could be for you. For some of us, we just couldn't think about that the first time around, and without much thought, we put the tree up as usual, whether it be an artificial or a real tree. Depending on the timing of your loved one's death, this can also be a factor on what you do or not do. Those that lose a loved one in late fall are confronted with the holidays a lot sooner that those that suffer the loss earlier in the year.

You may just go through the motions and try to do things as they used to be to just get through the holidays and think that next year, you will see where it takes you. And that is okay. Some of us may have an agenda already planned and decide that putting up the tree is too painful, and it just won't happen this year. And that is okay. Others may decide to replace the ornaments with all new ones and make it totally different than it ever was, while some will maintain the ornaments and allow the tree to represent the past with wonderful memories. Some people have ornaments that reflect their lives with their loved ones, and with Hallmark celebrating occasions with their ornaments, they can be very special to hold on to. And that is okay.

Bottom line is that what you decide to do with Christmas and the Christmas tree is entirely up to you and no one else. You have to be comfortable with how you feel at the time and what you feel like doing or not doing. There is no right or wrong way to do this. Be prepared for your feelings to change as Christmas comes every year because it can change how you look at things year after year. What you decide against one year might be a great idea next year. You may not put a tree up at all, then decide the next year you want the grandest tree you could find. Please know that it is up to you, and it is okay to feel and do what is best for you. Take care of you and don't worry about anyone else.

This season is a delicate one for those of us grieving the loss of a loved one, and it doesn't matter how many years it has been. There can still be a feeling of emptiness that we must deal with. Please know that you are not alone in this feeling because there are many others that share this with you. Look forward to making this season the best it can be for you, whether or not it includes a Christmas tree.

It is what it is, and what's best for you is what counts the most. Happy Holidays to you and yours.

Another New Year Is Here

The passage of time is marked in so many ways for us—birthdays, anniversaries, seasons, holidays, and New Year's Day. As time passes, we realize that life changes, and we move forward one step at a time. For those of us that have lost a loved one, time is an important aspect and significant mark for us.

The New Year signifies a "start over" for so many or even a means of measurement of our progress on our journey of grief. We struggle with looking back at the past year or past years without them, knowing that life was different for us and will now continue to be different for us as the New Year begins.

For some, the New Year will be the first year that you will begin without them, and the pain and emotions that you are feeling are still very much raw with sadness. You can't even begin to separate yourself from the facts of what happened or yourself from once being part of a couple with the spouse or significant other you loved. This is okay and is a normal feeling that you are experiencing. Please know that as each New Year rolls along, things will improve for you.

For others, this New Year marks another one of many that have passed without our loved ones, and in some ways, the feelings that we are experiencing have changed. We tend to feel a sense of separation from the loss that has occurred. Distance is becoming more prevalent from the time of the loss. And that is okay and a normal feeling. We are learning to move forward with positive insight, and the New Year marks achievement and progress in our journey. This is a time to realize that you are in the healing process, and it is becoming clearer to you that your path of life is becoming your new normal.

You will forever cherish the memories of your loved one and will not forget the impact that they have had on your being, but you will become stronger in identifying the person you have now become and will not feel guilty or inappropriate about enjoying life all over again.

Every New Year allows us an opportunity to look forward, to begin again, to settle old ways of life and start anew, to learn from the past, and to reflect on where life can take us in the future. Those of us that are survivors of the death of a spouse or significant other are no different than anyone else greeting the New Year. We all have the same opportunity to change our attitude, look ahead, and own the life we now have and make it the best that it could be.

I wish all of you a Happy New Year filled with comfort and peace.

As Time Goes By

I have had many birthdays since she died. The first few after her death were the hardest for me, and as each passed, I still had this realization that she is not with me to celebrate another year of me getting older. She will forever be forty-eight to me, her last birthday that was celebrated three days before her death.

We were to grow old together or so the desire was as a happily married couple, but she didn't keep her part of the bargain. Sue left this world far too soon. I was the same age as her when she died but for only four more months. And then that first birthday of mine would come, and I would advance a year by myself for the first time in thirty years of us being together.

The lonesomeness one experiences on a birthday for one after your better half dies cannot be described in writing. The sadness is overwhelming. Those of you that know that feeling understand this.

I listen to the songs that we shared. I watch the movies that we liked. I remember all the places that we traveled. I cherish all the time we spent raising our daughter. And now I am alone at a milestone, and it hurts more than I can say.

Our daughter is getting married, and only one of us is here in person to experience it. It's not supposed to happen this way. No daughter should be without her mother on her wedding day. No father should be without his wife on their child's wedding day. And yet it happens, not just to me but to many people out there, and it is sad and it breaks your heart. I know my wife will be with us, in spirit, on our daughter's wedding day.

It takes many years to heal after the death of your spouse, and in many ways, although you feel better about yourself and the new life you have redefined for yourself, there is still so much emotion that is part of your being. Every now and then, when the timing is right and life is happening, it comes to the surface, and it makes you cry.

That part of grief stays with you and will always be with you. The good thing is that it is not always present in that way, and it shouldn't be. If it is there after many years of grieving, you need to seek more help with your journey, and I encourage you to do so. Call someone, see a therapist or support group. There are so many others out there that know your pain and are there to validate your feelings.

Another birthday is a few months away for me as I write these words, and I am better with it coming and going after these many years. As I continue to get older without her, the meaning of life is changing for me. And as my life is lived daily and time goes by with life events concerning you and those around you as friends and family, one has to learn to acknowledge and accept those changes in experiences however hurtful they may be.

Everyone's life changes after the death of a loved one. Some changes are minor, while others are more prominent, but there is change. Change is inevitable in life's journey. You have to embrace it and accept it in order to continue to move forward, with faith and hope becoming your guiding light in your being…*as time goes by.*

This article was written two weeks before my daughter's wedding. Amanda became a beautiful bride and was wed on February 22, 2014, to the man of her dreams. Next to my own wedding day and Amanda's birth, it was the happiest moment of my life.

Two "If's" Make a Right

It was the heart of the '70s, and I was just starting college with an intended plan of obtaining a degree and beginning a career. I never imagined going into this adventure that I would not only meet someone to fall in love with but would marry that same person a month after graduation.

I did earn that degree I was intending to do as well as find my wife. Alvernia University turned out to be responsible for the beginning of my personal and professional life. To this day and perhaps forever more, the campus of Alvernia holds a special place in my heart. Over the years, I have returned many times even from great distances to find comfort and peace and have become involved in a teaching capacity as well as in their alumni activities.

Like many couples, we (my wife, Sue, and I) had a song. It was "If" by the group Bread, and in the day we listened to it on a 45 rpm or an album. It was also given plenty of air time on the radio when the group was popular with other hits. Our song stayed with us throughout our lives, and it was often played randomly at times when we would be together. It was at this time that life would stop for us, and we would look into each other's eyes and reflect, embrace, and kiss. It was tender moments like that which I miss to this day.

My wife's father passed away early on in our marriage when our daughter was still a child. He was a great man with sincerity, kindness, and integrity and held a special place in his heart for his daughter, my wife. Likewise, it can be expressed that Sue held a special place in her heart for her dad, and on one of his birthdays, she had his favorite poem handwritten in a beautiful font and framed for him.

It was only after his death and her request to have this framed poetry as a remembrance of him and his belief in the poem did I know about this. The poem is called "If" by Rudyard Kipling, and it is about a father's message to his son. It is a beautiful expression of life's moments and how best to handle them. "If" by Bread is a beautiful love song expressing the support and love two people can have for one another. Although two different ideas, both have the same title and shared within our lives together.

"If," the song, is still "our song" and one that gives me chills when I hear it on an oldies station or play it with intent from a Best of Bread CD I have. "If," the framed poem, hangs with warmth in my home, and I often stand before it and read it out loud, and it gives me the same kind of chills.

If only life didn't turn out the way it did, Sue would still have her father, and I would still have Sue. What I do have is representations of two "If's," one hanging on a wall depicting the love between a daughter and her father and one in the format of a song shared by a couple in love many years ago. Both "If's" make a right and will forever be in my heart.

It Might Be You

I smile at the sunshine, I enjoy a long walk, and I have fun with the dog...
It might be you.

I laugh at a joke, I read a great novel, and I feel good today...
It might be you.

I listen to music, I hum in the shower, and I sit on the deck...
It might be you.

I watch a good movie, I write my thoughts, and I enjoy the smell of the rain...
It might be you.

I take a ride in the country, I drink coffee, and I read the Sunday newspaper...
It might be you.

I have dinner with a friend, I walk in the park, I meditate at the lake...
It might be you.

I work on a project, I address a card, I help another...
It might be you.

I take a nap, I go to the mall, and I talk to our daughter...
It might be you.

All I do and All I am are influenced by you. I feel you with me day and night. I know you are guiding me, encouraging me and loving me as I continue on without you. I have learned to live with the loss of you. I will never forget you.

Living with It

It comes as fast as an unpredictable thunderstorm and catches you completely off guard. It hurts your heart and brings numbness to your soul. Your eyes well up with tears, and you begin to cry. You feel empty, your heart aches, and you want to be alone right now.

Something brought it on, and you struggle to figure out what. Sometimes you know, sometimes you don't, and that's okay. But for whatever reason, you are experiencing an emotion connecting you to the loss of a loved one.

This happens throughout the rest of your life, sometimes harder than other times, but there is a potential for it to happen to you any-time, anywhere. There is no stopping it or controlling it. It is now a part of you, and you have to learn to *live with it*.

Living with it can be challenging. You think that it should not happen after three, seven, or even ten years, but it does and may con-tinue to follow you as you move forward with your life.

Most people don't understand this unless they also have experi-enced this and have lost a loved one that was so much a part of their life. The love that we had for them never went away, and we continue to love them for being the person they were for us. Some of us still feel their presence, say their name out loud when we are alone, talk with them as we lie in bed at night, seek advice and guidance about the life we now lead without them.

They continue to be a part of our lives, living in our hearts and subconscious and occupying our souls with their love for us.

They want us to be happy and not to dwell on their passing and our loss of them.

Time passes, and over the years, it is hard not to be affected by a trigger of some kind that will bring back a memory of an event from the past you shared with them. It makes you miss them all over again, and at times, it feels like it just happened, even though time and reality tells us it was long ago.

Time is an equal opportunity employer. All of us have exactly the same number of hours and minutes every day. Wealthy people can't buy more time. Scientists can't invent new minutes. And you can't save time to spend on another day. (*Author Unknown*)

Using your time wisely and allowing yourself to experience the occasional thunderstorm, knowing that there is a silver lining out there ahead of you, makes good sense. The harshness of your hurt will pass like the thunderstorm, and you will feel good again. Don't dwell on the whys and feel bad for yourself. You are not alone in this. It's all about *living with it*.

Forgiveness

The beginning of the New Year can be daunting for anyone. Society encourages us to look closely at ourselves and chart a plan of action toward improvements with resolutions and real goals to become a better person. For most of us, resolutions made become resolutions lost.

People tend to hold onto things that anger them. And this feeling, for some of us, stays with us a long time. We hold on to it. We keep it in our minds. We never let it go. We hurt from it, and we will not be the same because of it. We can't forgive ourselves or apply forgiveness for the reason of our anger or discontent. *Forgiveness* can be a New Year's resolution, one that *can* be kept.

Losing a loved one can produce anger, disappointment, resentment, and even hatred for a situation or a person or even a business. And these feelings can run the spectrum. From being a little bothered to an intense anger, we can become full of rage against the subject of our discontent.

You can be angry at the person that has died for many reasons, one being that you are now alone without them. It is now up to you to continue on raising children, paying bills, trying to keep the house, and maintain the sanity that is left within you.

You can be angry at the medical profession for not saving or doing enough to save your loved one, from the actual hospital and staff to those that are still searching for a cure of a disease.

You can be angry at your loved one's organs that failed them— heart, lungs, kidneys, brain. You can be angry at a business or employer that was responsible for the death due to negligence or unsafe practices.

You can be angry at your own religious and spiritual beliefs, including your God. You can be angry at family and friends. You can be angry at an individual that you believe was directly related to the death of your loved one.

You can be angry at yourself for not knowing or realizing or being able to control something that you wish you could have controlled, even though reality dictates that it was totally out of your control. All of this anger is bad for you, and in most cases, being angry will not change the situation that has occurred.

Not forgiving breeds anger, hostility, and hatred. Being angry and not forgiving will allow you to continue living in the past and not being current to the present day. I know. I've been there. You don't even know that you are angry and are filled with hatred because it is so much inside you and part of your being. You just know you are not yourself, and it hurts. And you see so much of life around you in a depressed and sad way. It's not an easy task to forgive.

As C. S. Lewis once said, "Everyone says that forgiveness is a lovely idea until they have something to forgive." It took me a long six years to forgive the one person responsible for my wife's death. Afterward, I reflected on the time I wasted *not forgiving*. And it is not just something that you just do. You have to believe in yourself and your true feelings, and you have to want to do it.

Holding onto anger and distaste keeps you angry and depressed about what happened to your loved one, and concentrating on that all the time prevents you from living again. I felt it was time to move forward and become whole again. I was so tired of not feeling right about me or my life. Once done, you can begin to move ahead a little at a time and build your life again.

I never thought I would forgive, but I realized how not forgiving was destroying who I am and who I wanted to be. I did not like that I was angry and resentful to the world. I started to understand that being that way was keeping me stalled in life's path. I needed to move forward and become free again to do and choose what I wanted. Staying angry kept me confined and uncomfortable with myself and the world around me.

Forgiveness opens your world with possibilities of living again without the burden of the past holding you back. You will feel "lighter" and more at ease to move forward. You will look at life through the eyes of hope instead of despair.

So as we begin a new year, let's look for hope and faith in ourselves and select *forgiveness* as a New Year's resolution for whatever we need to forgive. I know you will feel better about yourself and the life that surrounds you. Happy New Year.

Community of Hope

A loss is a loss is a loss is a loss...there are no comparisons of one loss of a loved one to another's loss of a loved one. Any loss, anyhow, anywhere is sad, hurtful, and difficult to cope with and accept as happening to us. It can be a spouse, significant other, partner, child, mother, father, aunts, uncles, grandparents, friends, colleagues, and pets.

And unfortunately, at times, there can be multiple losses in a short period of time.

Any survivor of such a loss has something in common with everyone else that is struggling with losing someone or something you love. Each one's journey is different, but there are similarities. We share the hardship of the moment and the lack of future events that will not take place. We share the sadness and, at times, the guilt and anger that we experience.

The "we" becomes more so when we become part of a bereavement support group. It is here that we can be ourselves among others that understand. We can say things without fear of repercussions or receiving odd looks and insensitive remarks. We can open up and cry about our feelings and our search for a better day to come for ourselves. We are not judged here. We feel a level of comfort within the group, and being part of this experience allows us to realize that we are not alone with this problem. We are members of an exclusive club that no one wants to be part of, a club of grievers that are trying to make sense of our feelings and our roller-coaster ride of emotions. We are all trying to move forward one step at a time after the unthinkable has happened to us.

We become one with each other. We get it. We can be there for each other. And we can become a little bit better each and every day. Sometimes we don't even realize that we are making progress, but we are. Other group members see it better than we do ourselves. We look toward tomorrow with faith and hope. We seek encouragement and the renewal of ourselves to eventually become a reality.

Bereavement support groups—they can make a difference in your life becoming your own once again, and they are a community of *hope* for each other.

Silent Pain

We walk among you, unknown and not noticed, hiding behind the mask that we wear more often than not to the rest of the world. We are people that you are in contact with occasionally, or perhaps daily, within your circle of life. You may know our name and a little bit about us, but you really don't know us or what kind of pain we carry within our hearts.

Our pain is silent to you and only loud to ourselves. We are your neighbors, coworkers, or even the person you see walking past your house every now and then. We are the cashier at the convenience store or the delivery driver or perhaps your mailman. We can be the clerk at the front desk of the hotel you stayed at or the maid who cleaned your room. We can be your doctor or dentist, perhaps the last flight attendant you were in contact with.

Silent pain lives in silent homes, maybe a home with a pet or two. In our neighborhood, we wave or nod to you when we see you, and you return the gesture. Both of us are afraid about starting that conversation between us. And both of us wonder about the other. Early mornings and late nights, we find solace in the sound of the television or radio.

We lost a loved one, and although it was very painful in the beginning, things have improved for us to better handle things after some time, but the pain is still there, and at times, it comes to the surface very easily for us.

We feel marked, and we keep silent because we don't want to hear the response you are going to give us when you first hear, nor do we want your sympathy. We actually feel bad when you feel bad for us, so we are silent.

Communicating among us happens in support groups, if we have the courage to attend one. It is the one place we feel better about ourselves. We feel safe and understood, no judgments. And we can reveal our pain and shed the silence we keep among others that don't understand with those that do.

The very familiarity of one's intimacy with grief heightens its poignancy for others. (Mayor, *The Catch*)

We become sensitive to people that probe us with questions and don't have the decency to let us be and allow us to grieve in our own way and at our own pace. If we don't have the courage for a group experience, talking with someone who understands can help ease the pain, such as another person who also lost a loved one or a professional therapist or counselor. Another big step to take, but it does help you along your way after some time.

You begin to self-evaluate and realize that all of life is not lost. When tragedy strikes us, we see things differently from that point on. Any tragedy puts us in a different place. Our perspective and attitude changes, goals get reassigned, and priorities change. There is so much more out there that you can contribute to and to help others while helping yourself.

Life is for the living, and you must learn to live again and free yourself from the *silent pain* that has been keeping you hidden from other people.

After You

I never dreamed that there would be an "after you." There was a "before you," and I remember that well because my life was missing something. Then you came along, and it became "we." Both of us like the "we" that was created, and neither one of us thought of the possibility that the "we" would ever *not* be a "we."

No one thinks that. No one that is involved in a loving relationship thinks that or believes that it can happen. It is just *not* something to be thought of. Life happens and time passes, and all the joys that you both share continue and become part of your lives and your memories together.

It happened to me as it did for so many people before me and so many more people yet to be. I lost a loved one. My wife died way too soon, and this tragedy was very difficult to deal with for many years. And I had to deal with "after you."

What is now going to happen to me *after you*? What would my future be *after you*? How will I live again *after you*? How different will my life be *after you*? What am I going to do *after you*? Where will my life lead *after you*? Who am I now *after you*? Can I survive *after you*?

These are a few of the questions I pondered that needed answers. And you just can't consult a family member, a friend, a book, a website, or social media to find the answers. The answers to these questions about your destiny are within you. It will take time, patience, and reflection to find them.

There *is* life after the death of a loved one. It doesn't seem that way at first when your world is turned upside down, and you feel that there is no hope for you. Seeking help for you is an important step in the healing process. Many of us don't think we need this, but in reality, we all do. Look in the newspaper, search online, ask a friend, call a hospital, library, funeral home and inquire about a bereavement support group or a therapist or counselor to help you help yourself through this grief journey ahead of you.

Just talking out loud about what you are going through and hearing your own words will make you feel better and allow those listening to know where you are in your journey and provide the comfort you need as you move forward.

Eventually, one step at a time, you will know what is going to happen to you. You will know your future and feel good about it. You will live again. You will understand the change in your life for yourself and those around you. You will see a new direction that your life will lead you to. You will become a *new* you using the inspiration, love, and encouragement that you gained from your loved one to move forward with your life and feel a new sense of purpose. You will be a survivor of this loss and, in time, will look back and reflect how far you have come. I have been able to acknowledge, adapt, and accept what has happened to me *after you.*

Because of you, life matters after you.

I Miss the Mother of My Daughter

Those of you that have lost your wife, husband, or significant other and have children know what I am expressing here—from a two-parent/guardian household to one trying to cope and looking for answers. Life continues without them with you *alone* as the "parent" or "guardian" or "responsible adult person that can be asked questions."

Each person's situation is very different and is dependent on the age of the children at the time of the death, and I am sure we can all agree there is no "right" age or "right" time for this kind of tragedy to become part of our world and have us try to deal with "what now?"

On a personal note, so many life transitions and changes have occurred since my wife's death, my own as well as my daughter. My daughter was about twenty-three when her mom died, six months away from getting her master's degree and beginning a career. And there was no Mom to be proud of her. Her first move into an apartment, her first real job out of college—and there was no Mom to be proud of her. Her second move to another state and another job, her pursuit of more education—and there was no Mom to be proud of her. Her falling in love with someone to be part of her life, her engagement, marriage, and becoming a mother herself—and there was no mom to be proud of her.

I have difficulty knowing how empty my daughter's life must be knowing that her mother stopped being a physical part of her life at such a young age, and as she continues with new challenges and milestones, it hurts me that I can't be the mom for her. Her mom would know exactly what to say and do in any situation involving our daughter. Fathers usually listen to the mom and are grateful that someone is more in touch with their daughter than they can ever be.

I love my daughter and would do anything I can to help her along in life with her family, but I can't be the mom, and it really puts me in distress at times. Many of you have dealt with this situation and feelings of isolation from your children because the other parent or person is not there to balance the couple that you once were.

If your children are young, it becomes even harder to cope with trying to find the words to answer the questions they are asking and then dealing with everything involved in being a single parent or guardian. It's not easy. It is what it is. We do our best.

I am proud of my daughter who is now thirty-three. I know she knows I am here for her for anything, but I am not the mother that would be more comfortable for her to talk with, laugh with, seek advice from, shop with, have lunch with. I am the father who has faith and hope that every day, her mother is watching over her, guiding her and loving her spiritually as she lives her life with her family.

I am sure my daughter misses her mother, and I know *I miss the mother of my daughter.*

Entries from My Journal

There are times when my feelings change daily or multiple times a day, and I don't know why. Sometimes it feels like every day of my life is surviving until the next day, then it repeats again.

A few warm days, and you can feel it. The season is changing, and with it comes many thoughts and memories. I miss her. I miss her sharing the changes with me. I miss making plans with one another. I miss dreaming together.

It's not fun getting old alone. It's not supposed to be that way. We were united as one and now die separately, and one of us is left alone. I wonder if it was me that left first, how would she be handling this? I guess that will never be known.

I am allowing myself to be more "real" to me. This is all new, feelings that I have power over the present of who I am. I just want to "be" and slowly build myself up again to whatever feels right.

Sometimes in the middle of the night as I come out of a deep sleep and readjust in bed and close my eyes, I really believe I am not alone in bed. I recall and think that she is still here, and when I reach out, no one is.

I miss my old life with Sue. At times it seems that it never happened, and my past life is what I am today. And I really know that it isn't so, but it can be so believable at times.

Sometimes I believe that my life will never be settled again. It was stable and complete for thirty years with Sue and then my life as I knew it ended. And it's been up in the air ever since.

It's much easier to let go of material things, and only three years ago, I couldn't do that. Sometimes it takes a big change, like moving, to make you realize how much you have grown in a short time.

I hope and pray for a light that will show me the way out of this thing called grief and allow me to go in another direction, a direction that will lead to happiness and joy again.

There are things I need to do and things that I want to become. It's all about choices and allowing ourselves to make them without fear and regret.

I don't have nor will I ever have a person so loving and caring for me as Sue was. She brought such joy to my life in the simplest of ways. She could always make me smile.

I came across some greeting cards today that I received from friends and family and remember how I felt when I opened them. I wonder if most people realize how helpful and meaningful it is to receive a card in the mail from someone.

It could very well be the only thing that makes them smile that day.

Every New Year provides me with an opportunity to get a little bit better being the person I am and the person I want to eventually be.

I am one of many silent and alone widowers and widows who struggle each day without the one we truly love.

My life has taken a different course since the loss of my wife; I often wonder what it would have been like if her death never happened.

After many years of being a widower, I still feel alone and empty when new "firsts" occur in my life no matter how trivial they are.

My constant is Hal as he has been since the day she died. Hal only had a few years and some months to spend with Sue, but the rest of his years was helping me survive without her.

We don't realize how losses affect our lives many years later or how they altered our future outlook on life in general.

I have had to change my life and its destiny to fit my desires to feel alive again in some way, but in most cases, it's temporary until I feel the urge to make another change.

I've taken on being comforted by being at the park with Hal and just "being" while staring at nature and into the abyss.

III

Anxieties

One never knows how many anxieties or fears will become part of your survival after the loss of your spouse. We are all different in what triggers we experience, and so much is dependent on your environment and many other factors.

Here are a few of mine.

Any accident scene on the road I am traveling. Since I found out about my wife's death as I stumbled on the accident scene and saw right in front of me all of the many things that are associated with a traffic fatality investigation, any time I came across this familiar scene, I had an anxiety attack. I didn't even have to be driving; just as a passenger in a car, and it still happened to me. The flashing lights, police, fire, medical vehicles, caution tape, cones, first responders, fire police directing traffic, flares, twisted vehicle wreckage, tow trucks, tire skids on asphalt, and even the sound of radio communications and the smell of metal, gas, grease, etc. Since that fateful day, it took me ten years to be able to return to that intersection to make any progress in my well-being.

Tractor trailers. This was the means by which a distracted driver took my wife's life as well as a part of mine. I felt anxious while driving on the same road with them. I couldn't stop seeing them daily on the roads I traveled or in the parking lot where I worked. It wasn't until after I retired about four years later that this anxiety began to dissipate.

Mondays. Sue died on a Monday, the sixteenth of the month, so Mondays were an issue for me. Unfortunately, they came once a week, and it was a day that was filled with anxiety for me because it was a *Monday*, the day of the week that she was killed. I even couldn't think Monday and thought of it and later labeled it as *pre-Tuesday.* At one point, I even counted the Mondays that passed, so I had a running total of what numbered Monday just passed that not only had she died but I was without her. Also, whenever the sixteenth of the month fell on a Monday any time in the future, additional anxiety was felt, and at times, knowing that it was coming made me want to be off that day, so taking a personal day or a vacation day from work was something I often did. This went on for years.

Work/office. I was at work in my office when I answered my phone to talk with Sue's boss who was calling me to inquire about Sue's not showing for work that afternoon. This phone call began my search for Sue and wondering about her whereabouts. Since my world as I knew it changed at my work and in my office, it was something that stayed with me and provided such anxiety to me going forward every day afterward when I went to work. These feelings haunted me till the day I retired from my job forty-three months later.

Time, 2:40 p.m. The time of the phone call from Sue's boss. This froze in my mind and would be a constant reminder in countless ways to me over the next five years. There were times that certain things happened during the course of a day that highlighted that time, or I would wake up for no apparent reason in the middle of the night and would look at the clock, and it would read 2:40 a.m. References to that number even came to me in license plates of cars that were in front of me to lottery numbers drawn. If I was in the office on a Monday afternoon, and it was getting close to that time, I would leave the office for a walk to avoid the phone ringing at 2:40 p.m. As the years went by, it became less frequent, but to this day, occasionally, it still happens.

My house. We spent about seventeen years at the house we lived in, so needless to say, I saw my wife everywhere in and outside of that house. Most things in the house were things she wanted or purchased or decorated. Her taste and presence was everywhere. This can be both comforting as well as problematic at times. It was difficult to remain there and still move forward, so I felt the need to move and do something totally different with my life.

Hospitals. I was driven to the hospital by first responders from the accident scene. It was there that the finality of it all came together within my scattered mind. Time stood still there, and there are things about it I don't remember, but the fact that I was in an emergency room at the local hospital to identify my wife's lifeless body was a bit more than I could bear. I feared that hospital and would not even drive on the same street that it was on. Years later, a friend called who wanted me to meet him at the emergency room to provide support to him while he was dealing with some health issues with his wife. I dropped what I was doing, hopped into the car, and started to drive to that very same hospital when it struck me. I pulled over and had an anxiety attack and was shaking and crying, knowing the last time I was there was that day Sue died. I did continue on and did get to the hospital to help my friend but not without extreme anxiety and a few sleepless nights later.

My sister's van. My sister and brother-in-law came to my house the day of the accident and supplied the transportation I needed to meet my daughter at an arranged place half the distance between my home and her university. I needed her close to me and, as we rode in the van to this meeting place, I was in the front passenger seat while my sister was in the back and her husband drove. Many times after this, when I was visiting my sister, and we would take that van, I would get anxiety especially when I was seated in the front passenger seat as that day going to meet my daughter.

My father's death. My father died approximately two months before my wife. On the anniversary of my father's death every year, I think that when he died, Sue was alive, and little did either of us realize that she would be killed two months later. I am not sure if I ever did process my father's death since shortly after, I lost my wife. I also think of my mother dealing with the death of her best friend and husband, my dad, then months later, having her son lose his wife.

My daughter crying on the phone. It was the most difficult phone call I would ever be part of in my life, telling your child that their mother is dead. My daughter was away at college, and five hours separated us. There is no good way to do this. Her reaction and sobbing on the phone without my physical presence to be next to her, to hug her, to be there for her was the most sickening feeling I ever experienced in my life. To this day, when my daughter is sad on the phone or is shedding tears, that experience haunts me.

Change—Phase II

Sometimes it felt that I was on some kind of cycle. And it seemed to be labeled as the three Rs—*reflect, regroup, relocate*. In a second set of circumstances, I was facing this challenge again.

After finishing what I had to do, it was time for me to move onto another chapter of my life, and once again, after reflecting and regrouping, it was time to relocate. This time I was in a better place emotionally than I ever had been, and it was from this past adventure that placed me there. I was guided by an inner voice, gut feeling, or maybe my own consciousness. These guides got me here and now were taking me elsewhere, back to Pennsylvania.

I always enjoyed the act of "being." No matter where you are, you have the choice to just "be"—be in the moment, relax, meditate, reflect on your surroundings, cleanse your mind of worries and concerns, and be present with you. I can just "be" when I do something I enjoy doing or if I am with someone I enjoy being with. I can also just "be" when I teach or when I write. I am not sure if I ever experienced this act of being before my wife died? I did meditate before from her suggestion to help solve my migraine problems, which it did, but the other feelings associated with "being" were not there for me, or at least, I didn't acknowledge them like I do now.

Part of experiencing change is to have courage to *want* to move forward. Once that is achieved, it is a little bit easier to begin to achieve. Along with courage is taking risks. Sometimes it takes longer than we want it to for us to be comfortable with taking risks as we try to move forward. If you don't develop courage and take risks at some point of your journey, change will continue to be out of your reach, and you will miss out on living life as you try to move forward.

Unfortunately, our society still does not give death its due, nor does society allow the survivors of the loss to just experience it the way they need to. In most cases, you may get the day off for the service; if you are lucky, maybe three days. And according to society and most of those around us, we go back to life as if what just happened was merely a bump in the road.

Recovery from any loss is time consuming and all-consuming as well. I believe that you are always on that mission of recovery, never really being totally recovered from the event that changed your life. Recovery takes many forms and involves many experiences and situations. Recovery can include but is not limited to visiting the past, searching one's soul, meeting new people, talking with strangers, thinking out loud, writing your thoughts, sharing with friends, sitting in silence, thinking, planning, doing. At times I think you are never done recovering from an event that turned your world as you knew it upside down. You are just on this road of progression toward a better day. You are making progress, as slow as it seems sometimes. You may not even notice it because you are too close to you, but those around you do, and it is nice to hear them acknowledge how far you have come because it is at that time that you begin to believe it yourself. Once that happens, you have more confidence in what you can do and be, and then an increased sense of hope and faith fall into place.

Recovery can happen by itself, but it takes much longer. Helping the recovery along the way is where the real progress can take place. Counseling, therapy, support groups all have their place in your recovery, but that has to be your choice. And this kind of outside support is not for everyone. They are something that you have to pursue; it is not just going to happen to you. Hopefully, there is someone that is part of your life that will recommend or tell you about participating in one of these or all of them. It cannot hurt to be a part of one of them. I personally could not have made it without them.

On the pages that follow will be reflections that I wrote to share with others through my newsletter and other newsletters since my wife died. There will also be a selection of entries from my personal journal that will follow the reflections. Most of the reflections and entries have appeared in the quarterly newsletter of *sudSSpirit*.

Reflections

Revisiting the Past to Find Peace

It was Martin Luther King Jr Day in January of 2006. I was in my office on a typical Monday afternoon. The phone rang as it usually did dozens of times a day, but this phone call that came in at 2:40 p.m. would be the beginning of the end of my life as I knew it. As I answered the phone, I had no idea what was about to unfold in front of me.

The phone call alerted me that my wife didn't show up for her part-time job. I took the usual steps of calling home and her cell phone with no answer, followed by a visit to the house which appeared in order and her car not present. Thinking that she had car problems and was in an area where there was no cell coverage, I proceeded to take the route she usually took to go to work, thinking I would find her broken down somewhere.

I did find her, but she was the sole fatality in a horrific traffic accident involving a tractor trailer driver who was speeding and ran a red light. The truck pushed her car into a building on one of the corners of that intersection. She just celebrated her forty-eighth birthday three days ago. She died instantly. I died a little that day too.

I was in shock for what seemed like an eternity. The trauma of losing your spouse suddenly and unexpectedly took its toll on me and turned my life upside down. What was I to do now? Where was my life going without her? Why did this happen to me, to her? Everything in my life changed, and I felt I had no future, no identity. Nothing mattered anymore.

I knew I needed help and searched for it. I went to a general bereavement support group for six weeks. I sought out and attended one-on-one counseling from a therapist for a number of years. I continued to seek out and attend bereavement support groups monthly. I read as many books as I could find on bereavement, grief, losing a spouse, etc. The librarian knew me by my first name. I began to journal. I cried—a lot. I also created a bereavement support group to help me help others in the same boat I was in.

I decided to retire from my career, not feeling part of the corporate world anymore. I sought out a new beginning for myself. I sold my house and relocated to another state where I bought a home and opened a business. The relocation helped me move forward emotionally in ways I didn't know I needed to. It was then that I decided to move back.

Throughout all this time without my wife and even with the many steps I took to help myself through this life-changing event, there was one issue that I could not resolve. On that fateful day in 2006, I stumbled on the accident scene where my wife died. The scene before me was forever etched in my mind's eye—first responder vehicles, police and fire personnel, flashing emergency lights, caution tape and orange cones, fire police directing traffic, closed roads, twisted wreckage of vehicles, scents of oil, gas, and metal, sounds of mumbled voices, a scene of chaos where you knew death was present. That was the last time I was at that intersection, with no desire to return to it ever again.

Finding out about the fate of my wife this way—my own discovery of her accident scene—I would not wish on anyone. This visual experience before me would haunt me every time I came across an accident scene from that point on…for the next ten years. I would shut down physically and emotionally and have to allow myself time to process the scene for about ten minutes before I felt comfortable enough to continue driving. I wondered at times if I would spend the rest of my life having to cope with this vision of the past tragedy that took my wife away from me.

Fast-forward ten years to the day: January 16, 2016.

My thoughts are that this is the final piece to that awful time of my life, the memory of how that scene looked when I stumbled on it that day to realize that the love of my life was no more. The visual of that intersection and its surroundings with all the horror around it and how I revisited it in my mind every time I saw an accident scene needed to go away, and I needed to find a way to heal from that nightmare.

I thought of this for years that the only way to find some kind of peace from the shocking sight of that accident scene was to revisit the scene someday as it appears normal. I never felt comfortable or ready to tackle this issue until now.

I asked a good friend of mine for a huge favor—to be available on January 16 and be willing to drive me to the site and be silent as I observe, walk, reflect, cry, and do whatever it is I had to do to find a sense of peace and comfort from an intersection that was in disarray ten years ago to one that was normal and functioning as it should be. I warned him that I didn't even know how I would react that day, and everything was up in the air at this point, but I felt the need and the desire to try. Worse case, he may have to drive me to a hospital should I become light-headed or experience a severe anxiety attack.

I met my friend at a parking lot about five miles away from the intersection. I felt confident in myself after preparing for the last few weeks with meditation and de-stressing techniques. Upon arrival at the location, I took in the view and everything around it—buildings, businesses, traffic, people walking around.

I exited the vehicle and walked around two corners of the inter-section, just observing the normal functioning of the intersection, hearing muffled conversations of people and the sound of traffic moving and stopping at the traffic signal. I watched as the scene in front of me had no trauma or sadness, no fatalities or closed roads, no flashing lights or uniformed first responders, and I took a deep breath and closed my eyes capturing the moment.

I felt good, positive, warm and comforted. I felt like a weight was lifted off my shoulders. I walked back to the car and joined my friend. I spoke about how I felt and how this visit seemed to help me. He drove me back to my car.

It's never too late to try to better yourself with your grief journey. You will know when it is time to take another step. Trust your instincts. I knew I could never revisit that intersection until I was ready. It took me ten years to be ready, and doing this on the same day of the accident many years later made it even more worthwhile to me.

This was a life-changing moment for me, facing my fear and winning. I experienced a kind of consolation from doing this. I am at peace in that respect finally.

Taking a Bike Ride with a Memory or Two

On a beautiful Sunday afternoon when the weather was too nice not to be outdoors, I decided on a bike ride on a trail near my home. Many others had the same idea as I pulled into the crowded trailhead parking lot—couples, families, some pets too along to enjoy the sunshine. A mix of walkers and joggers were also present.

Bike rides are different for me now—solo. My wife and I rode our bikes together on many bike trails around the current home we were occupying at the time. When our daughter came along, and she was able, she accompanied us. For many years, this was a favorite pastime, sharing the outdoors with the ones you love, doing something healthy and fun.

As time passed and my daughter matured, she did not want to be part of the Mom/Dad bike ride, so it came down to the two of us, and that was okay. Years later, with knee trouble, my wife dropped out and then took up kayaking. We would then drive to a lake that also had bike trails, and although we did separate healthy and fun things, we enjoyed the drive to and from and then the conversation of how our experience was.

As I biked on this mostly shaded trail today, this is what I was remembering: our talks, laughs, betting who could get to the next marker first and seeing who could be less out of breath. Memories like it were just yesterday; happy and fun memories of times passed.

I smiled and said hello to so many people that were on the trail today, thinking of the times they were sharing with each other at that moment as a couple or with children, whether walking or biking. I also thought of those that were by themselves like me, men and women alone, taking a walk, jogging, or bike riding. What's their story? Time alone from their spouse or family, single, divorced, widowed—maybe they were reflecting the same thing I was.

Riding my bike now has a new meaning for me, a good one. I have come so far on my journey and still enjoy riding a bike. It provides a sense of freedom and allows me to think and remember all the good times I shared with my wife and daughter. I am comforted with being on a trail and out among nature, feeling content and satisfied. I am so happy for those moments and all the other moments I shared with them. It is so important to spend time with those you love right now. Time is something that when taken away, can never be returned to you. Enjoy your time and create moments with your loved ones.

Life is defined in moments... I am glad that there were these past moments in my life so that I can have fond memories now.

From the Way We Were to the Who I Am

Webster's dictionary defines *transition* as "a passing from one condition, place, etc. to another." Most transitions eventually can be defined as a transformation—change the form or condition of. That is kind of what happens when a transition from *we* to *I* occurs.

I am one of many who experienced a transition in their life when my wife died suddenly and unexpectedly many years ago. The transformation was sudden and unexpected as well, and I certainly wasn't looking forward to what was about to become a reality. It was frightening. It was uncertain. It was a transformation I wasn't ready for. But who could be?

In those early days of the tragedy, I wasn't sure how I would survive day to day, let alone months or years later. So many thoughts and emotions and feelings of helplessness and hopelessness occupied most of my time, and I could not control it or stop it from happening to me. I was transformed into a world I knew nothing about, a world without the love of my life who had been there for me for some thirty years.

I began to journal my thoughts. I sought out and attended a bereavement support group. I went to a therapist for one-on-one counseling. I applied forgiveness. And all of that helped me understand where I was and provided me with searching my own soul to determine where I needed to be and how I needed to get there.

I was blessed with resources that most people don't have to take huge risks and big moves to help my journey of rediscovery. Through leaps and bounds that brought me through some low valleys, I survived when it was all said and done. I learned from my adventure and grew as an individual and became someone that I would have never recognized before the journey began.

I can only speak for myself but offer to you that in order to move forward with one's life after a tragedy, you have to be willing to take chances, make choices, and forgive. And even if they don't work to your satisfaction, it may have taken you to a place that will help you later in life. You may not know that at the time, but it will become apparent in the future.

It is amazing what the human spirit, a good attitude, and a positive outlook can do for you. It may feel like the world came crashing down upon you, and there are cloudy skies with a storm brewing, but you have to go through all of that in order to see the sun again and, if you are lucky, a rainbow too.

You can't stay in a place of sorrow. You must make the transition from *the way we were to the who I am* and accept the new transformation of the new you, a person who wants to live, laugh, and love again and become the best that you can be for you and the friends and family around you. I am a survivor. Shouldn't you be one too?

I Could See It in Your Eyes

Today was her birthday. She would have been fifty-nine. Her last birthday was followed by her untimely death three days later. Everyone who knew her knows the impact her death had on them and remembers her departure from this earth as being so sudden, unexpected, and devastating.

I can't avoid being sad on this day and the days that follow. And it's not just me that experiences this low point. Her friends, family, former coworkers, and even you are feeling the pain that goes along with the sadness.

You had very little time with her before she died, Hal. The time you did have with her made a huge impact on her, and it is clear that your love for her was beyond being measured.

They say a dog's eyes are so humanlike, and at times, one thinks they really understand your moods and feelings and respond to your needs with a comforting paw, a tilt of the head, or the look in their eyes.

I could see it in your eyes today, Hal. *You* are giving me a look that speaks volumes that you miss her as much as I do. You sense my sadness and in turn validates your own loss of her companionship and love. I got down on the carpet with you, and we consoled each other just like we did on the night of her death—you and me, alone, missing the one person that we loved so much.

After her death, your life changed as did mine. She was such a part of our lives, and being without her these many years still hurts like it just happened. *You* know what this day is. You know that three days later she died, and neither of us could believe that this was for real. We've been through this year after year on the anniversary of her birthday followed by the anniversary of her death.

This year, you and I really connected, Hal. You truly do understand and grieve as I do and miss her and love her. It's been the two of us continuing on with each other's support. But I must admit that what you offer me is far more than what I offer you. Since I'm the talker I pour out my soul to you through words, tears, and hugs. And although you can't say a word back, I know you understand, support, and love me. I can see it in your eyes.

Man's best friend is more than just a pet. They are more than a friend. They are part of a family, your family. They are there for all that you experience (happy or sad) and ask nothing in return. Their unconditional support and love is never-ending, their loyalty and trust unmatchable. Their presence in your home welcomes you, comforts you, provides peace to you.

Of all the dogs that were part of my life, you are one of a kind, a companion to me for the last eleven years. You fall into the category of "one in a million" just like she did. And there will never be another *you.*

It's Time to Cut the Grass

One of the first signs of spring is the grass getting greener. When that happens, it usually is accompanied by the grass growing as well. This prompts what most people don't look forward to—cutting the grass.

Once you start, you must keep performing this weekly ritual throughout the spring and into the summer and even early fall. This task just about covers parts of three seasons. No wonder it is so grueling and disliked by many.

I have never really liked cutting the grass and really admire those that do this task for a living every day all day long, sometimes seven days a week.

I like to be the last person to partake of the first cut of the season, at least in the neighborhood, and in most cases, I do become the "last man standing." It's silly, but it made a chore become a game to begin the grass cutting season.

There is more to this story than grass cutting and my dislike of doing it. As Paul Harvey used to say; "Here's the rest of the story."

From the first blade of grass I cut till I was finished with the lawn, I always looked forward to coming into the house and seeing my wife there. There would be small talk and maybe a glance out the window by her with a comment about how good the grass looked since it was cut.

I would make a comment how hot it was or it went faster this time than usual or even some difficulties that I had with the lawn mower this time around. It was just chatter between us, and it happened every time I cut the grass over the many years no matter where we lived at the time. It was something between us that was as common as breathing is; you just don't realize you're doing it, but it is done.

It was that chatter that made my grass cutting bearable, and it made it fun for me, just like being the last man standing. I'd like to think that it was fun for my wife, Sue, as well, or she did it because she knew it pleased me. As other married couples can attest to, we did things to please each other knowing we are making them smile.

The small talk is no more and hasn't been for many years since my wife died. I miss the chatter and that common ground we shared after I completed such a mundane task of cutting the grass. As some people say, sometimes you don't miss something until it is no longer there.

The first time I cut the grass after her death was very difficult for me. When I finished, I did not want to go into the house right away knowing the silence that awaited me. I puttered around the yard and rearranged the shed. I even began cleaning up the shrubbery beds which is a task I detest. I eventually got enough courage and walked in and dealt with the heartache I knew was coming. I cried while sitting in my favorite chair until there were no more tears to shed.

Each year became a little easier to deal with this, but it is difficult to not think about it even to this day. Sometimes it's those little things that mean nothing to no one else but you and your spouse that you remember the most with the fondest of memories. I smile now after I come into the house after cutting the grass, almost hearing her voice and our exchange of small talk. I miss you, Sue.

We All Have a Story

Losing a loved one can make us feel all alone. We feel like it has happened to us and only us and that no one else out there understands what we are going through. Some of our friends stop calling, and at times it seems they are trying to avoid us when we really need them to be there for us. Not everyone handles the grief of another in the way we would like them to. And it is not their fault. Our society has trouble understanding and acknowledging grief and all that it encompasses.

Your personal story of tragedy is yours alone, but one must realize that *we all have a story.* Knowing that there are others that have stories of the loss of a loved one allows us to realize that we are not alone. Although everyone's story is different in many ways, the true similarities come forward when they are being shared among the attendees of a bereavement support group.

People with similar losses will have similar feelings and will be able to identify with each other with their feelings. A bond among them will be created, and it is at that moment that you realize in a very small way that you have something in common within the grief process that is happening among you.

Seeing a therapist or counselor one on one or in a group is also very helpful during the bereavement process. Telling one's story is what it's all about. During appointments with trained professionals, what you express allows the listener to comment and pose questions to you that allow you to search your own being and reflect on what is happening within you at the time. After some time, you begin to reflect on your own and are able to turn your negative feelings into positive actions of moving forward.

Telling our story helps us. Each time it is told, whether in detail or a short summary, allows us to express and hear our own words in our voice tell how it is. This provides acknowledgment and comfort to us. This empowers us. This telling of our story becomes easier with time, and we recognize how helpful it is over time.

It may be difficult to share with others, especially the others that are strangers to you in a group setting. Trust me. The strangers that are gathered hurting from a loss like you are will become friends that come together to share thoughts and feelings. Together, you will be there for each other, and together, you can help each other heal.

We all have a story…share yours today.

Memories

Even without triggers, we like to recall past events and make them be present with us. We like to look at pictures, handle an item or two, remember a scent, a look, a smile, the way a voice sounded. It can even be how the wind blows on certain days that make us remember or the warmth of a sunset or sunrise that brings on a memory.

Being among nature can have many effects on us too—sounds of wind blowing through a forest or a brook flowing against rocks, sounds of the ocean or birds singing. Everyday noises that are usually distractions can also be a gateway into a world full of past memorable moments.

Just the past weekend, I came across two obscure happenings, old songs and T-shirts. I came across a cassette of old songs that we shared a love for. I played it, and it happened to me. The memories came flowing back, beautiful loving memories of times past. So vivid they were I could actually envision us (my wife and I) together. It was wonderful.

I also was going through dresser drawers and came across T-shirts, T-shirts that were significant of a time and a place, where we were or what we were attending, a souvenir of a past event that brought back those memories like it was yesterday. Some of these were mine, and others were hers that I had to keep and still love having. I wear them to this day, and it makes me smile when I see them and wear them knowing what they represent for both of us and especially why they mean more to me than ever before.

It doesn't matter how you come across memories. It matters that you continue to have them and use them to your advantage of remembering a happy time when you were together. Be thankful for building those memories with your loved one and still celebrating them to this day.

The Best That You Can Do

One of the most difficult issues I have been dealing with since my wife, Sue, died is my search for where I should be in life, not just where in terms of what I should be doing and for what purpose but also the where in terms of geographical location, a struggle that I have yet to conquer, but I keep trying.

One never knows the contentment and satisfaction one feels with their life until a life-changing moment occurs like the death of your spouse or significant other, and then you have to rethink your future all over again. Your world turned upside down, the rug was pulled out from under you, a physical and mental challenge to your body and mindset as to what do you do now.

At times I think I am the only one with this problem or, at least, the only one that is this distraught over this effect it has on me and how much time I spend dwelling on it. Others I have spoken to are coming along fine, maintaining their daily schedules and lives and pretty much are where they have been but minus the one they loved so dear. I am happy for them. Others have made some changes. Perhaps they relocated to another home or apartment, moved to another town to be closer to family, or moved in with another person. I am happy for them also.

I have accepted my grief journey. I have accepted what has happened to me, and I strive to help others with their journeys of grief, but I have not accepted where I should be or what I should be doing or where I should be doing it. People I speak to about this dilemma of mine say that I am searching for something that does not exist. Others say that my searching is what I am doing and is where I should be; meeting new people, helping others, relocating, trying new things, learning, exploring, writing, sharing. Be happy with the present, the now, they say. Don't overthink it.

I am not sure what the answer is, if there is an answer. I sometimes think that I am overthinking it, but I can't deny that I feel like something is missing in my life, something tangible as well as spiritual, and that is "this search" I speak about.

I have made so many changes and decisions. I have allowed myself to explore, create, meet head on, switch, become vulnerable, take risks, cry, laugh, express, and pray. Some of the things I planned out methodically, while others were spur-of-the-moment ideas that I carried out to see what would happen. Whatever the case, no regrets. I did it, and doing it made me feel worthwhile and in control of my own destiny, for that moment in time.

And then I needed more. It seems I am never content with where I am and what I am doing. I look back at my life with my spouse, and I was very content with where I was, sharing a life with her. Am I looking for that missing piece that I lost when I lost her? And after this many years, should I finally realize that I will never be able to duplicate that?

So what's the answer? Is there an answer? Is this really a problem? It can be one man's search for a destiny he has yet to encounter. Will the search be endless? Perhaps the search should never end for the search is part of the life I now lead.

Whatever the future holds for me, I know that change is inevitable, and nothing really stays the same. A common expression voiced by many is this: "It is what it is, but it will become what you make it."

As this New Year begins, I wish you all peace and comfort in your own personal journeys.

My Best Friend Is Now in a Better Place

I knew him for fifteen years. No one knew me like he did. We both shared something—we lost a loved one twelve years prior, a loved one that was such an important part of our life was gone forever, in an unexpected instant. That sudden loss was traumatic for both of us. Neither of us knew what we were going to do or where our life was taking us going forward. It was scary. We both were in sorrow in our own ways but there for each other to find peace and solace.

We became dependent on one another. We knew that each other needed the other more now than ever before, and we became closer than ever before as a team and were part of everything together. He was so patient with me. He was understanding. He knew when I was sad. He comforted me when I cried. He made me smile and laugh out loud. He brought joy to my life. He was my dog. His name was Hal.

Hal wasn't always my dog. He was the dog of my wife, Sue, handpicked by her from a litter of pups in a home in Ohio. Hal was welcomed by both of us into our home. Sue wasted no time with training Hal. He was put through every training she could find and passed all with flying colors. Hal even herded sheep at a farm one time. He became part of agility training and was even in training to learn a game for dogs called fly ball.

His ultimate and most meaningful training for himself and his master was therapy dog training. Hal trained for and passed rigorous tests to be certified by two associations, one state and one national. Hal also became part of a therapy dog group as well as being on his own to visit those less fortunate. Sue and Hal visited hospitals, assisted living centers, nursing homes, and would even visit the elderly home alone to bring a little joy to their day. When talking about their day, Sue's face lit up with excitement, and Hal stood proud wagging his tail. I wasn't sure who enjoyed helping others more, Sue or Hal.

As ironic as it is, I became the recipient of a much-needed therapy dog after Sue's death, a therapy dog whose sole mission was to help me cope with the loss of my wife. I then became his therapy support person to help him deal with the loss of his master. For twelve years, we did everything together, each of us aging, along with many changes in both where we lived and what we did. We experienced multiple moves where we occupied three homes in two states, and my work schedule went from nothing to part time to more than full time, long hours, nights, and some weekends. He experienced new neighborhoods, new backyards, and new dog friends.

Hal went from having dog friends he saw weekly at a dog play group to being alone when I was away at work and lasting long hours at a time till we saw each other. He has been to many parks and walking trails, enjoying his time outdoors. Hal loved the snow and the cold and got his fill while we lived in Vermont. A local artist we met there actually painted Hal's portrait for me.

We shared a bond I never experienced before with any previous pet. Hal was the last being to see Sue before she died. She took him to the trail for a walk right before she left for work that day. Little did Hal or any of us know she would not return home—ever.

Hal gave me the best years of his life, and I would not be where I am today without his presence, support, and unconditional love. I have talked a lot about Hal to many people over the years, and so many of my friends and family know the role he played in my life. No one would question the devotion and caring attitude we had for each other.

Hal's kind eyes reflecting his soul provided peace and comfort to all. We were both together for that length of time to help one another and be there for each other. I will never forget you Hal. You will be forever in the hearts of those that knew you and loved you. Thank you for being there for me.

Hal: October 31, 2002–December 28, 2017

Letters to Heaven

I've been writing letters to heaven for a long time. My basic method is through journaling, plain and simple. But it doesn't have to be actual writing or writing in a journal. It could be through thoughts, wishes, hopes, even prayer. Whatever method, it's communication from you to whomever you are addressing your feelings to.

Communication through music and/or poetry can't be forgotten either. Many have written songs and expressed feelings through poems about the experiences they had with their loved ones or the experiences they have had since their parting. It's all good, healthy, and helpful. This provides an opportunity to say something you want to share about now or perhaps to say something you never got to say but you need to now.

I like to share events that are happening in my life at the moment, knowing that the one I lost is also experiencing it but in a different way, events that they are not a part of physically like they once were. I also use this time to ask questions about future decisions or seek guidance and acceptance, even direction or help with a problem. Feedback will not be vocalized, but I know I have received answers and direction in other ways. You have to believe, and you must be open to it.

There are times when my writing has turned into a diary of sorts, but that is okay because you are sharing thoughts and expressing feelings about your day without them, and it allows you to vent about life in writing. It provides a needed outlet for you where you are not judged and only you know what you have written since you control the privacy of your letters to heaven.

Writings can be all over the map with regard to context and emotion. Sometimes they are sad, while other times they are happy and carefree. No matter how you feel, it should be reduced to writing and expressing in communication of your thoughts and feelings. There is no pressure, no deadline, no rules when you pen a letter to heaven. It's you and your deciding what to write, when to write, and to whom to write to.

And it is up to you to decide to keep what you wrote or discard it, share it or keep it to yourself, look back to what you wrote before or never return to what you once wrote. You have total control. Control is definitely something that helps you to realize that there are things that you are capable of controlling. Knowing that you have control over something helps you feel better about life since most times, you are not in control of your own destiny or the destiny of others you love.

So put pen to paper or type on a computer. Create a poem or write a song. It really does make you feel better. I've been journaling for twelve-plus years and have filled dozens of journals with my thoughts and feelings. *Letters to heaven* are always welcome.

One Year Ends, Another Begins

It happens all too quickly, doesn't it? We begin a new year trying to keep resolutions, break bad habits, become a better person, and live life better than last year. We think we have an entire year to do it, and we do, but time gets away from us without us even realizing it.

Before we know it, seasons change numerous times, birthdays come and go, and the year is half over only for us to say "where did the time go?" We concentrate on the second half of the year, and time keeps ticking away, leading us into the last quarter of the year with seasons changing and the holidays. Then *one year ends; another begins.*

Time is one of those things that when gone, you can never get it back. Just like losing a loved one; once they depart from our world, they will not be physically seen again here.

As I write these thoughts, it's December, and I am going through some containers of Christmas decorations. Most of which have a story of when purchased by who and where and how we (my wife and I) enjoyed sharing in the joy that they bring. I discover a few programs from Christmas plays that we attended, the last one being her last Christmas, 2005. We loved to attend plays at local theaters, and five years prior, Sue heard about this one theater group in Harrisburg, Pennsylvania. We decided to go to their Christmas play every December after that first one we attended. They were all good and well done, and it became a tradition.

The next day after the play that December, I purchased tickets in advance for the next Christmas performance in 2006. I got front row seats and was going to surprise her when the time came. The time came, but I attended the play alone since her death happened approximately three weeks after that last Christmas play we saw together. I sat in the front row with an empty seat to my left and, in some way, felt her presence next to me.

I have Christmas songs playing as I go through these Christmas decorations and then realized that the CD I was playing was the CD that we always listened to in the car on our way to the Christmas play every year. Did I randomly select that one or was I helped?

Most of my days in December come and go without any sadness. It is at certain times and certain events and rituals that a somber moment is experienced but quickly dissipates with the wonder of the season and what it represents to all of us. I think of her daily and always will for the rest of my years.

I didn't get the tree as I write this, but next weekend that will happen. A real tree is a must that is adorned with many ornaments that we have accumulated over thirty years of a lifetime together. And each one has a story that I recollect as I place each one on every bough. This is a happy time for me as I think of how fortunate of a man I am that I met her, fell in love with her, married her, had a child with her, and spent the best years of my life with her. Sue left our world too soon, but I am grateful that she was part of my life and made my life what it became to be.

So the year is winding down, and into history it will go. We look forward to a new year whatever it may hold. We remember this past year that we have improved a bit in our daily lives along the way. We project faith and hope to guide us in the next twelve months. We won't take "time" for granted, and we'll use it as wisely as we can to improve ourselves and well-being, health, friendship, and new adventures.

Then before we know it, *one year ends, another begins.*

We may have experienced the *s*udden *u*nexpected *d*eath of our *S*pouse or significant other, but we are *S*urvivors in *p*articipation to *i*nform, *r*enew,_*i*mprove, and *t*riumph over what life has dealt us.

Happy New Year!

Reminiscing

I just left Michael's Crafts, having dropped off the last six items to be professionally framed. For the last three years, I have been taking treasures created by the hands of my wife, Sue, and have been giving them the credit and honor they deserve.

My wife was very talented in sewing, and when it came to counted cross stitch, her skill was second to none. She would not agree with me or anyone that tried to compliment her on her creativity and skill set. She never looked at her projects as being something to be admired by others. Sue was modest to a fault.

She worked part time for Dimensions. Dimensions was a business that sold kits for people to do on their own. Sue was the person that created the sample displayed on the walls for the customer to see what the finished project looked like. Besides a paycheck, she would receive a discount to purchase kits on her own. Sue created many beautiful things and would frame and mat some of them herself. Others she created never received a frame but remained stored away in a box somewhere.

In a way to honor and remember her, I've resurrected projects from boxes and took poorly framed treasures and provided them with a new look professionally done. Afterward, I would find a place on a wall within my home. At this writing, there are about eighteen of what I call treasures adorning my walls, one of a kind, made by her, priceless pieces of time and talent that have a special meaning to me.

I look at these daily and reflect of a time passed, a happy time where she enjoyed working on and completing each one of them. Seeing them gives me joy and comfort knowing her hands touched and created what they offer. In a way, doing this has been therapeutic for me, creating memories from memories but in a new perspective. Sometimes I enjoy taking them all in as I stroll around my home with a cup of coffee or a glass of wine in hand, like I am in some art studio looking at a personal collection.

Any of us that have lost a loved one wants to and does remember them. We all have different ways that we do this. It could be a one-time event, an annual celebration, or a daily ritual that brings them into our present world and makes us smile. Only we understand this desire.

Memories of our loved ones are priceless to us. We will always feel connected to them and look forward to any opportunity to talk about or reflect upon the life we had with them.

What's Your Status?

Single, engaged, married, separated, divorced, widow, widower—a question I dreaded being asked directly or responding to on a
form that I was asked to update for the first few years after the death
of my wife, Sue.

Being married twenty-five-plus years, it was hard to think of
yourself being anything but that—married. The cold reality was that
things changed, and I was now a widower but did not want to admit
that let alone own up to it. I wanted my life back to the way it was,
but what I wanted was impossible.

In those early years of grief, the many changes on paper that
one must go through are too many to deal with—banks, mortgages,
rental agreements, income taxes, shared ownership of cars, utility
bills, cell phones, homes, insurance policies, beneficiaries and, of
course, "in case of emergency, please notify…"

So often, the status of you is asked for verbally or on a form that
must be updated due to your new situation. And there are times you
are not really thinking about it till you're asked or you are provided a
clipboard at a doctor's office with a form to be completed, and there
it is, right at the top, "Status."

The first time this happened to me, I actually began to shed
tears as I looked at the form and read what it was asking me to do,
and the once-familiar check mark in the "Married" space was no
more. I remember leaving it blank because I did not want to check
"Widower." Luckily, the receptionist knew of my loss and never
asked, or she competed the check mark for me. I was lucky.

In other ways, it was not that simple. Trying to remove a name
off a cell phone was difficult; they actually wanted a copy of the
death certificate since Sue's name was on the account. Providing that
had its own difficulty for me, but I got through it.

Most times, those in the receiving end of the answer to your
question in person or on the phone are very kind and respectful, providing their sympathetic response and condolences. Sometimes even
then, I felt bad because they felt bad. In some of my past jobs, I was

the one asking for the status of a person not realizing the impact it may have on that person until now that it has happened to me, and I truly understand.

We all become different when our status changes, different in a positive way because now we get it and are understanding and more compassionate to others. Just like in grief, once we are in the thick of it, we become validated by others as we continue to validate those that are just beginning their journey.

Some of us have gone through this before, from married to separated or separated to divorce in sadder times and single to married in happier times. I suppose it depends on your own status and how it changes along with life changes that make us think about this.

So what's your status? After whatever life-changing situation that you have been through and now are acknowledging and adapting to it, maybe it should be *survivor*.

I Remember When

I remember when...

...We first met at college
...We walked in the snow together
...We had fun every Halloween
...We got engaged and then married

...We enjoyed movies
...We had fun traveling and exploring
...We sat by the fireplace
...We had our daughter and were so happy

...We moved many times for my job
...We made each other gifts for Christmas
...We celebrated our Anniversaries
...We picked apples together

...We attended plays together
...We bought our first home
...We planted a tree together
...We soaked in our hot tub together

...We had dinner out
...We bought our first new car
...We took long drives to new malls
...We first got HAL as our dog

...We went on picnics in state parks
...We kayaked on a lake
...We rode bikes on trails
...We worked out at home together

...We comforted each other in times of need
...We encouraged each other to go for it
...We smiled at the college graduation of our daughter
...We enjoyed our last Fall season together

...We celebrated her last Birthday
...We kissed for the last time
...We were so happy to be with one another
...We once were...and I will never forget her

Life Experiences

The experiences of life that we go through are as diverse as our individuality. There are some things some of us never experience, or we are limited to what we do experience, depending on our paths of life that we chose or were chosen for us. Some of us experience many things for the same reasons.

But no matter where you fall into this spectrum of life, whatever you experience makes you the person you are. Add to that the people around you while you are experiencing it, and that changes it up a little. Add the location that it is happening in as well as your age, and that increases the meaning behind it as well.

Life-changing situations can be either planned or unexpected. They can be hoped for, wished for, dreamed about, thought they will never happen, or prayed that they never come to be. We cannot control them as we cannot control life and our destiny.

So we think of those milestone in one's life and reflect—birthdays, birthdays that have more meaning (sixteen, eighteen, twenty-one, thirty, forty, fifty) youth sports leagues, first job, clubs in high school, dating, honors, awards, high school graduation, college life, dean's list, honors, awards, falling in love, college graduation, first job out of college, career decisions, getting married, having children, moving/relocating, changing jobs, divorce/separation, losing jobs, death of a friend, death of loved ones (parents, spouse, children).

These milestones, life experiences, happenings, life phases, or whatever you want to label them changes us in a small or large way. However this affects us, it does make a difference in our lives, a difference that is never really noticed at the time it is happening, but it is there, and it is making us different than we were before.

Any one of them can be a pivotal point in our life that enables us to change our outlook, attitude, and outcome for the present time and, at times, for the future.

As I reflect about one of my life-changing experiences, the one that changed everything, the sudden unexpected death of my wife, I can see how my world as I knew it ceased to exist, and another one took its place. I did not have a choice. It came fast and out of the blue, and I was right in the middle of it before I knew what really happened.

Everything changed—my attitude, opinions, thoughts, feelings, ambitions, desires, needs, wants, challenges, goals, what I thought about life, friends, family, colleagues, work, money, success, happiness, love, heartache, sex, friendship, charities, strangers. What was once important was no longer, and what was never thought about was always on my mind.

The changes in me as an individual did not happen all at once, nor were they seen by others right away. But they were there, and they were making me become someone I never was before. This new person I became was good and bad for me. When you are experiencing many changes in your being, you begin to have much self-doubt and uncertainty about your life and your future.

Eventually, you lose friends that were close to you and your spouse, people at work treat you differently, and new people that you meet are cautious about what to say and don't really know who you are. You are one, and you are alone. And one really is a lonely number, as the song implies. It becomes a balancing act. You're on a high wire, and there is no net below to save you. It's up to you to pursue and keep moving forward, one baby step at a time with no regrets.

This is also a new beginning for you, one that you have to create and do something with your newfound feelings and attitude about life and your future. I started to appreciate the little things more. I began to take no one for granted. I realized who the most important people in my life were. I finally knew what mattered and what was important about living and life. I began to take chances, take risks.

Each day is a gift as well as a risk. I shared my feelings more with people I liked and respected. I reached out to those I have not seen or heard from in a while. I searched for ways to contribute my talents and skills to causes and others in need. In a way, I kind of reinvented myself. As much as I liked the old me and did not want to leave who I once was, I knew that person left with the death of my wife, and there was no going back.

It may take years for you to realize all that I just said here, or perhaps you already have experienced some of this. Whatever the situation, please know that you are not alone in this. There are countless others going through the same thing. Life threw us a curve ball, and we are trying to hit one out of the park toward a brighter future.

The House Comes Alive Again

When the unimaginable occurs, and you lose your spouse or significant other, the home and its environs takes on a whole new meaning. The presence of your loved one is missing and not just temporarily. A void is present. Silence is deafening. Your purpose is misguided. There is no doubt that much has changed, and you could not avoid it.

You may be fortunate to have family members still residing with you, and that helps, but it is not the same. You may be lucky to have a pet or pets that require your attention and love while they help you cope with the missing person in your life. Sharing your place of residence is helpful to you, but again, it does not take the place of the terrible loss of your partner.

Some of us aren't as lucky and have neither family, friend, nor pet to share space with after the death of our loved one. This can be challenging and very quiet. The place you call home takes on a new feeling and sense of serenity. Serenity can be good, but too much of it during a weak moment can make the best of us feel awful and takes us in a downward spiral of despair temporarily. The still of the house and the quiet associated with it can indeed be disturbing at times, making one want to go out and be surrounded by sounds and other people to just maintain our sanity. You experience this and get used to it and find ways to cope with it.

That is where I've been at until a summer weekend visit from my daughter and her family. The house came alive again! My daughter lives in New England, and we don't get to see each other too often during the course of a year. So when she found some time to visit, I was very excited. The talk and banter among adults and the sights and sounds of an almost five-year-old along with their baby sister just lit up my world for the weekend. What a great feeling of love, belonging, and togetherness. Moments which were once of silence and serenity turned into laughter, games, and silly songs. Just being in their presence was the therapy needed to bring such joy into my heart.

I reflected for a moment the loss of their experience with their grandmother (my wife) whom they never met, but I did not remain in that mindset too long. I knew that in some spiritual way, she was present through my heart and was sharing in their visit.

Seeing my grandchildren enjoy themselves at the playground nearby and being part of their explorations of life took me to a happy place I have longed for these many years. A day full of fun at an amusement park followed by a trip to the pool enhanced the time together. Watching a Disney DVD together and just plain being silly created memories to cherish. What a way to uplift your mood and attitude.

The weekend ended, and so did their stay. They packed up and headed home. But not without hugs and happy memories. The house returns to its stillness and serenity, but the feeling I experienced will last me a long time knowing that there will be another return trip from them. I am looking forward to when I will take a road trip to see them, and the fun and laughter will continue.

Even Now

Even now,
You will smile at moments of recollection.

Even now,
You remember how they helped you in a difficult time.

Even now,
You remember their laugh, their voice, their touch.

Even now,
You remember the way they looked at you when you knew they
weren't happy.

Even now,
You remember their sadness and their own worry.

Even now,
You remember events, occasions, places you went together.

Even now,
You remember raising children together.

Even now,
You remember the quiet moments you shared.

Even now,
You remember walking in a park exploring nature together.

Even now,
You remember painting the bedroom together.

Even now,
You remember making breakfast or dinner together.

Even now,
There will never be a time you're not sad by their absence.

Even now,
There will never be a time that you don't remember them.

Even now,
They will always be part of your life.

Out of Touch

Hugging is a very comforting and communicative type of touch.

When a friend or family member is dealing with something painful or unpleasant in their lives, give them a hug. Scientists say that giving another person support through touch can reduce the stress of the person being comforted. It can even reduce the stress of the person doing the comforting.

A hug can indicate support, comfort, and consolation, particularly where words are insufficient. A hug usually demonstrates affection and emotional warmth, sometimes arising from joy or happiness when reunited with someone or seeing someone absent after a long time. In other situations, a hug can indicate familiarity, brotherhood, or sympathy.

An unexpected hug can be regarded as an invasion of a person's personal space, but if it is reciprocated, it is an indication that it is welcome. Not everyone likes hugs, and one must be cautious not to overstep one's bounds and create an uncomfortable moment, especially with people who dislike hugging.

After the loss of a spouse or significant other, we also lose touch. We are not touched as much, nor do we touch, hug, embrace as much. Yes, we lose another something. We may continue to touch, hug, but it will be few and far between and certainly not with the intimacy it once was with our loved one.

Being out of touch can make us feel isolated, lonely, and depressed. When was the last time someone touched your arm, shoulder, shook your hand, sat close to you, or provided a hug to you?

Hugging has been proven to have health benefits. One study has shown that hugs increase levels of oxytocin and reduce blood pressure. Oxytocin is a chemical in our bodies that scientists sometimes call the "cuddle hormone." This is because its levels rise when we hug, touch, or sit close to someone else. Oxytocin is associated with happiness and less stress.

The stress-reducing effects of hugging might also work to keep you healthier.

In one study of adults, researchers found that hugging may reduce the chance a person will get sick. The participants with a greater support system were less likely to get sick. And those with the greater support system who did get sick had less severe symptoms than those with little or no support system.

A group hug has been found to be a useful tool in group therapy to provide a sense of cohesion among the participants after a session, although it may cause discomfort for group members who shy away from physical contact. Please be cautious and respectful of others' wishes.

It has been found that touch can reduce anxiety in people with low self-esteem. Touch can also keep people from isolating themselves when reminded of their mortality. Unfortunately, some people today are touch-deprived. Many people live solitary or busy lives with reduced social interaction and touching.

Touch can also include the touching of a pet like a dog or cat. Many studies have proven the positive results that animals in our lives can bring to us in our time of need. I can personally support this with how my dog Hal got me through the many tough times after my wife Sue died. They also found that even touching an inanimate object—such as a teddy bear—helped reduce people's fears and anxiety.

Don't allow being "out of touch" get the best of you. If you feel nervous about seeking out more hugs, start by asking for them from friends and family members closest to you first.

Sunday Morning Walk

On a recent morning, after attending a local postcard and ephemera show, I decided to take a walk on a local trail. The trail I speak of is the Grings Mill trail that meanders along the Tulpehocken Creek and remains of the old Union Canal in the Reading, Pennsylvania, area.

It was good to be back there again, recalling the last time I was there alone was about nine years ago and, with my wife, Sue, more like fifteen. It was a favorite trail of ours that we often walked, rode bikes, took our daughter there with her bike, a family experience in many ways over the years.

As I ventured on this sunny morning, I said hello to many along the way—couples, singles, families that were enjoying the day as much as I was with walking, jogging and riding bikes. Sometimes, walking helps us clear our heads and provides a much-needed relaxation time spent with our own silence. The walk becomes effortless and not even tiring as we sort through our innermost thoughts about life around us. I felt myself smiling as I recalled fond memories of walks from the past, happy moments of time spent with my family along this trail, not knowing that there would be a day (this day) when I would be doing this very thing now.

I am grateful for the past that allowed me to share my life with someone I loved and to have been part of the experience of raising a daughter that my wife and I are so proud of. I know Sue knows that Amanda is doing fine as a mother of two and wife of someone she loves. I know Sue knows about her grandchildren and how precious they are to the family.

Being outdoors on a beautiful day can be inspiring. Adding to that a walk along a familiar trail that brings back warm memories can be satisfying. There are places along that trail that made me stop and reflect about things we spoke about, planned, and we even took a break on one of the benches along the way. Sometimes the walks along the trail took us to events that were scheduled along the trail for all of us to enjoy and become a part of the experience. As time passed, and we all grew older, our conversations changed, and eventually, our walks were the two of us since our daughter became of age where she would rather be with her friends.

I have been doing a lot of walking lately to stay healthy, and like most of us trying to lose a pound or two, most of my walks are in and around my neighborhood and, occasionally, along a bike path or trail. Walking is peaceful. Walking, when you do it daily, seems like it takes no time to complete. Before you know it, you just walked briskly for thirty minutes, and you're back where you began. It's like a meditation, a time of reflection, an opportunity to cleanse your mind of thoughts and worries and be in the moment. I do miss walking with Sue, but there are times I feel I'm not alone because I sense her presence around me and am comforted to know she will always be in my heart and soul.

Another First Many Years Later

It is often communicated from a variety of sources that the first year after losing a loved is difficult in that there are many "firsts" that will take place without them being there with you, for you. In most cases, that is true; however, the firsts *don't stop* after that year. Please don't be fooled by this.

Your life changes because life as you knew it changed. You may be going through things now alone for the first time. Perhaps the second or third year, you will decide to relocate to a more manageable apartment or home. You may decide to change insurance companies, cable companies, phone services, and you will now be making those decisions alone. Maybe you never did the finances, and now you are overwhelmed with paying bills and budgeting. It's not easy.

Decisions about your pets are made now by you. You may be at a point of needing a newer car, and you've never done that before… alone. The lawn mower stops working, or you are clueless how to start it or get it serviced. Many online sites and accounts are password protected, and that is something that has to be dealt with as well.

Fortunately, some of us have good support from family and friends to help guide us and provide feedback about our choices in whatever decision is before us. But ultimately, it is on you.

It's been over a decade since my wife, Sue, died. I would have thought I conquered "all" the firsts at this point in my journey of life without her. Not true. This past year, I had to go through two outpatient procedures that required me to be driven to and from the site. One of them, I never had done before, but it was just as much a trigger of emotions knowing my wife wasn't the one to be there. The other was a repeat procedure that I recalled my wife being the one that was there for me. That flashback affected me more. Two firsts within a year, many years after her death.

I am blessed and fortunate that my sister and brother-in-law were there for me during those times. I am grateful for their time, compassion, and caring attitude to make me as comfortable as they can during those moments. I struggled with these incidents being *"another first,"* but what choice did I have?

So my message to you is that all those firsts in life without your spouse or significant other can come along despite the time frame of your grief journey. Only you have the power of acceptance, acceptance of what life is now for you and believing that you can get through whatever the future holds for you.

Nothing Stays the Same

Change is something that we love and hate. Many of us need change and need it often. We're not satisfied with the way things are for too long and must make a change to something else, something different, something newer, something easier. That's our choice. Some of us like the way things are and hope change doesn't happen. We want it to be the same, and we don't invite change. We're satisfied and happy with what we are, what we have, who we're with, and where we live. That's our choice.

There are those of us that are a little of both. We like the way things are but are not afraid or reluctant to a change here and there. Our thoughts are that change is good, sometimes. When something remains the same, life becomes stale, stagnant, boring. Some of us require change more often and dislike when things stay the same too long. Desiring change often makes life interesting, exciting, adventurous, and it challenges our souls to keep up with ourselves, our drive.

When examining our life and taking the time to reflect on where we have been and where we are now, it will become clear that *nothing stays the same.*

In spite of ourselves and our willingness to be the master of our destiny, it doesn't matter. Change is inevitable. Change will happen. Change is part of life. It's difficult for us to accept something that we have no control over, like the changes in our lives that happen suddenly and unexpectedly. This kind of change is not our choice.

My wife Sue died suddenly and unexpectedly, and believe me, everything changed. Life as I once knew it stopped. And it took years for a restart. The new beginning for me was just that—all new. I never had to think about life without her since I met her in college some thirty years ago. Change was happening, and it was noticeable and at times uncontrollable. None of us in a loving and healthy relationship think it's ever going to end, even though we all know that death is the final act of life.

Nothing stays the same for any of us during what we call normal times because life happens, and choices are made. When tragedy strikes, it's all hands on deck. Death changes everything. Each baby step you take puts you in another place and a different state of mind, less of who you once were and more of somebody you don't even know yet. What you do, where you work, how you live, who you talk to, what you believe, how you feel, why you hurt, how you express yourself can all change.

Most times these changes are happening so fast and being driven by uncertainty, emotion, fear of the unknown, and the desire to feel better than you do right at that moment. You're in shock. And you will be for some time. It's tough to be grounded at all. I remember saying to myself and, at times, repeatedly out loud to those around me "I don't know what to do." And I didn't. I was clueless.

There are things that have to be dealt with in a timely manner, and they come first. And you are reminded of them by those that require you to do them. That is priority. Everything else is secondary and later, much later. As time passes, and you begin to feel some sense of togetherness, you slowly begin to function in a basic fundamental way. This is where the changes come in, and hopefully, you will be able to think about them with some sense of clarity.

Change will project you into a future of unknowns, a future of who you will now be. You are no longer the person you once were—when you had your spouse with you. Some of us will wait at least a year or more before making any real big changes, while others are ready way before then. It is really up to the individual, and most times, it is encouraged, when in doubt, to seek advice from a trusted friend, family member, or professional.

I don't know of anyone that has been through losing a spouse that hasn't changed the way they look at life. Many changed their lives through relocations, career changes, retirement, volunteering, faith, hope, prayer, journaling, helping others, peace, exploration, and attitude. Whatever changed for you, beware. Another change may be coming because *nothing stays the same.*

So Many Lives within a Lifetime

You only live once. In my previous life. Such is life. Life happens. Life is like a novel. It's filled with suspense. You have no idea what is going to happen until you turn the page.

The other day, I was with a few friends, and one of them made reference to the way something was handled where he had worked before, and he prefaced it with these words, "In my previous life, we did it this way." Everyone knew the reference point being of a past time, past employer, or past career. It made me think that we all have those moments in life that are like a totally different life than where we are right now. And those previous moments constitute many lives that we experienced.

Life is what you make it. Life goes on. Life doesn't stop for anybody. Let me live my life. Death is not the opposite of life but a part of it. Life is a gift.

So thinking of it that way, how many lives will we have in a lifetime? If I share my own list, I guess my first "life" was the life I had growing up with parents and a sibling, friends in the neighborhood to friends at school till high school graduation. My second "life" happened when I went to college, and for those four years with new friends and experiences, I grew as an adult, met the girl of my dreams, and fell in love. Life number three is when I got married to the girl I met in life number two. My third "life" ended with her death; therefore, I am starting a fourth "life," a life without her.

Life will break you. This life's hard. Life is about not knowing. Life is pain, highness. Enjoy your life. Accept what life offers you. It's your life.

There are also sub-lives within lives that enhance our beings and character like when or if we became a father or mother, an aunt or uncle, grandparent. Changing jobs or relocating or starting a hobby can be a sub-life within a life. My teaching experience was part of my third and fourth life, therefore, being part of two lives. Opening a business was a sub-life for me as was entering a new career in social services. Retirement is a sub-life for many of us.

Life flashes before your eyes. Life is for the living. Live the life of your dreams. One of life's lessons is always moving on. It's okay to look back to see how far you've come, but keep moving forward.

None of us have just one life if you look at it this way, and our life doesn't end when we lose our spouse or significant other. Of course, none of us that have would ever be convinced of that when it first happened, myself included. That's where the healing process of time comes in, time that provides us with wisdom and rationality.

Don't take life too seriously. Life is a series of natural and spontaneous changes. Our life is what our thoughts make it. Life is funny. Things change, people change, but you will always be you.

Whatever numbered life we're on, we're living a life with purpose, kindness, appreciation, compassion, and understanding. We've become wiser, experienced, friendlier, and forgiving. We find ways to cope, believe, have faith, and hope. And we move forward knowing how richer all of our lives have become from spending the time we had with the one we loved.

Everyone you meet is a part of your journey, but not all of them are meant to stay in your life. Some people are just passing through to bring you gifts, either they're blessings or lessons.

Entries from My Journal

Reflecting, remembering, and reliving moments from my past life with my wife and realizing how lucky I am to have shared them with her.

As I write, I realize that it sucks when something great happens to you, and there's no loved one to share it with you or be happy about it with you. It's just you, alone, in an empty house, and for a moment you wonder if something *really great* did happen?

Music is such an emotional connection for me in so many ways. I listened to a cassette tape I made for Sue with her favorite songs, and I smiled all the way through them. Miss you.

There is still a daily presence around me of her love and support for me. I am so blessed to feel this and acknowledge it and to know that her spirit lives within me.

No one can talk and express their feelings better like those that are grieving. Everyone in the group, even those that I saw for the first time, know how I feel, and I know how they feel.

I miss her. I miss the blueness of her eyes, her laugh, the scent of her hair. I miss sharing life with her because now life has another meaning—foreign in many ways—so different, so complicated, so uncertain.

I wonder if what I am doing now in this stage of my life is what I want or need to do right now. I've learned how life can end so abruptly, so I want to make the most of my time doing the things I love to do.

We are a different kind of group or club, those of us that lost a loved one—a spouse or significant other. We are unique because of the past experiences that we had with them and the future times that will never be.

I really think you tend to think about your loved one more after they have died than when they were alive. It's odd to say that or think it, but I feel like I'm doing that. When they are present, you know you will see them and take that for granted. Afterward, you'll never see them again.

Hal's death was and continues to be very difficult for me. I must believe he is no longer in pain and discomfort. I also want to believe in the rainbow bridge and that Hal is reunited with his master, and he is happy and healthy once again on the other side.

The length of time that has passed doesn't change your thinking of them daily. It strengthens your desire to keep them remembered and honored, always loved, never to be forgotten.

My heart aches knowing that my grandchildren will never know and enjoy the love of their grandmother.

Each year adds to the new memory column of AD (after death) as opposed to those cherished past memories of BD (before death) with my wife.

For whatever reason, I opened one of two memory boxes packed by both of us in 1997. I cried, remembered, and smiled. It's nice to know that they are there for whenever I need them to be.

Every year brings on the reality of you not here and not coming back and the difficulty of my continuing without you. I think of you every day because you never left my heart.

I miss my old life. It left the day she died. The world I knew stopped that day, never to spin the same speed again. Nothing stays the same—ever. Life's outlook and your future within it are redefined by how you accept it and deal with it all.

All my life without her is a task—one that is always a challenge for me—and each step deserves a reflection of where I've been, how far I've come, and where I have yet to be.

This grief journey that I am on has forced me to consider that all the lives around us are so often taken for granted, but each one is burdened with its own troubles and heartache.

No coffee today. I decided to have tea—loose tea in a mug Sue liked with a picture of a sheltie on it. I felt the need to have tea on her birthday, in her honor, a celebration of her life—a life that made my life so wonderful.

I've grown without you in ways I've never seen coming; some good, some lonely, some confusing but always missing you and your love for me.

IV

The Finality of it All

Would you want to know when the "end" was, the end of your life? How different we would all act knowing this, or would some of us not act any differently?

The year 2005 was the last full year for my wife, Sue. She didn't know that, nor did I. When I look back at that year, we did so much together that I am thankful for. Come to think of it, we did a lot together for the thirty years that we knew each other, and that was special.

Three days after my wife turned forty-eight, she died. It was sudden, unexpected, and the result of someone's negligence behind the wheel of a tractor trailer. The driver was speeding and ran a red light one afternoon in January 2006. She died of blunt force trauma to the chest after the truck hit her vehicle broadside and pushed her car into the porch of a building at an intersection.

I died a little that day too. My world was upside down. I could not believe that this was happening to me. It was like a dream or, more so, a nightmare, one that would not end, and I couldn't wake up to see that none of this was really happening. But it was real, and it did happen. And I did not know what to do.

Life stopped. Anything I was, anything I knew, any thoughts I had did not exist. I was in limbo somewhere in a vacuum of time where no one could find me, and I could not find myself.

When I thought back to the final full year, 2005, I can't help but think of all the "lasts" that are now part of the memory and the history of us—the last spring we shared, my last birthday with her (when I turned forty-eight) Memorial Day weekend, the last summer, our last wedding anniversary, Fourth of July holiday, the last fall, Halloween, Thanksgiving, and Christmas holidays.

The year 2006. As every new year comes into play, as with all of us, it is to be better—new hope, new beginnings, new experiences. But this new year for us was to be defined much differently—her leaving this world and me trying to survive this world without her.

I don't remember a lot about the beginnings of this journey I was on, and that may be a good thing. I do remember some things that I wish I could forget—the accident scene that I stumbled on "by accident," my daughter crying hysterically on the phone when hearing the news of her mother's death, and the sadness and depression of her dog, Hal, after he realized she was not coming home—ever.

Time Passes. Life Continues.

None of us really think about life ending. We are all caught up in our own worlds every moment of every day. And we have many worlds, but none of us define them; they just are there. We exist daily in such a variety of worlds that they run together and at times collide. We never see it coming, but when it happens, we notice that things are more difficult. We get frustrated and angry and feel shortchanged in what life has to offer us.

We never consider how we could change things though. We just keep going and going and going. Eventually, our worlds will collide once more, and we keep the pace as before. And such is life in the fast lane, a lane that most of us share with one another because we all do it. Days blend into each other, and weekends that we longed for are over before we know it. Spending time with our children is on a long list of things to do, and unfortunately, their time is way after so much more that we prioritized. Spending time with our spouse or significant other is far down that list as well.

Months fly by, seasons change, holidays come and go, and we are still on that treadmill of life as we know it. As years come to an end and new ones begin, we notice how fast our children are growing up, our hair is thinning or going gray, and our soul mate looks as worn out and tired as we do when we glance into the mirror of our souls.

So where does this take us? We hope we are able to become successful and happy and live a life of promise with those that we love, but at what cost? All that time in the fast lane too often burns us out before we even get to enjoy the life we have with those that matter most to us.

Time. It is the one thing that when taken away can never really be given back. It's lost. Gone. And we regret its loss more than anything else that we lose. The loss of time to do something, complete something, say something, attend something, visit someone, go somewhere, the loss of time to spend more time. We always want more time and yet don't take the time to plan better to have more time. We never really structure our time with the most important of our priorities.

Losing a loved one refocuses our attention on time. We begin to see time in a different light. We see how time is so important to spend it with those you love and to cherish the time we have with them. Our goals change from what they once were. We use the time we have more wisely. We want time to move quickly to get over the sad feelings we are experiencing, yet don't want to lose track of time or forget about the loved one that died.

We also want time to move slowly because we are not ready to make decisions about our own new lives without our loved ones. We are just not capable yet of taking some steps, and we want time to slow down to give us more time to think about what we want to do.

Time *passing* occurs for all of us, and it is up to us to do our best to manage the time we are given. We all have the same amount of time each and every day. We must make a choice how to use our time.

Time moves on, and *change* is inevitable. We have to seek out and explore new beginnings, new traditions, new attitudes, and a new us without losing sight of where we came from and the contribution to our lives that our loved one provided to us to make us the person we are today. Use your time wisely for the good of yourself and those that are part of your life.

None of us realize that each day is a gift, a gift to make a difference in our own lives as well as the lives of others, a gift to cherish, share with others, and being content knowing that at the end of the day, it is wonderful to be alive and well. I know now, but do you?

It's not too late to start caring more, loving more, believing more. It's not too late to *not* take your loved ones for granted. It's not too late to spend more of your time with those that you love and feel good about being with. It's not too late to be more kind to anyone and everyone that crosses your path. It's not too late to have hope and faith and peace within yourself. It's not too late to be thankful and humbled by what you have.

My Grief Time Line

This is my personal grief time line, what I felt, how I handled my feelings, and the actions I took. How someone else reacts to their own grief may be a totally different experience.

2006: Shock and awe

This first year felt like I was in a twilight zone. Nothing seemed real. I was going through the motions of everyday life without knowing what I was doing, who I was, or where I was going. I was in a forever nightmare, not realizing any kind of reality of the situation I was in, and everyone around me was distant to my needs. I wasn't even sure what my needs were. I began to write my feelings on three-by-five cards nightly.

2007: Pain and fear of uncertainty (hardest year for me)

Reality came hard to me this year. After the initial shock from the past year, I now realized that my wife was gone and not coming back, and I had to face the life ahead of me without her. We knew each other for thirty years, married for twenty-six and a half of those. I began to journal.

2008: Limbo, what do I do now?

I was attending bereavement support groups and individual therapy but felt I needed to do more for myself and others like me. I started a bereavement support group and began to write about my feelings and share with others. I felt I was in a place between where I was and where I have yet to be, an uncharted territory of my life that I never expected to be in. I was clueless to what was ahead of me or what I needed to do with my life.

2009: Choice / change / leave the past

I found it increasingly difficult to continue working at my career and felt that I needed a change. Working in my position didn't feel right with my wife gone. She did not work with me, but not having her support took me in a different direction. Near the end of this year, I retired from a career in retail loss prevention and took some time to decide what was next for me.

2010: Continue and adapt to change; some things work, some don't; keep moving forward

As I thought about what was next, I still taught part time at a local university (something I've been doing for the last twenty-four years). I thought about relocating to another state and do something totally different and then decided to do that late summer of this year. I also felt that my relocation was needed to make me move forward. At the time, I wasn't sure what "forward" meant.

2011: "New Normal" begins… Rocky road but happening. I was able to forgive. (Six years Later)

I am in a new state, bought a home and a small business, and began something "new." I attended a bereavement support group and then decided to start a chapter of my bereavement support group. Being in a new place, meeting new people, and doing something different helped me focus on myself. I was able to determine some of my anxiety and deep-seated anger I was hiding was not allowing me to be in a better place. I challenged myself to forgive the driver of the truck for his negligence in ending my wife's life and part of my own life.

2012: "New Normal" established. Time for new changes, adapting to change and choices became easier, going forward.

Forgiveness is a wonderful thing if you can do it. I am sure I would have never been able to realize the need to do this or have the strength to do it had I not relocated. My heart and disposition opened up so much. Working in a small business and being focused elsewhere helped me go forward. During this year, it became apparent that the business was failing, and I had to close. I stayed where I was and moved the business to my home and online.

2013: Regroup, reflect, relocate

The online business became more of a hobby with less sales, and I searched for teaching employment at local colleges. Thoughts of returning to Pennsylvania began to cross my mind, and later in the year, I moved back.

2014–2015: Continue to revisit places that had meaning for me and for us while experiencing reflection, renewal

I began teaching part time again and became more involved with volunteering. I also found I had the need to go to places that made me remember happy times with my wife. This provided me with a sense of renewal and peace.

2016: Facing my fear ten years later

January 16, 2016, I revisited the accident site for the first time. I needed to see it "normal" without the wreckage, first responders, flashing lights, orange cones, and no fatalities.

Afterward, for the first time in ten years, I can now drive by an accident scene without the need to pull over and cry. What I now do is pray that no one lost their life and no one is going through what I did. I began a second career in social services and continued to volunteer.

2017: Another loss

October 16, 2017, Hal, at age 15, had multiple seizures, and his health began to decline.

December, 28, 2017, Hal crossed the rainbow bridge and joined my wife, Sue. I am now truly alone for the first time.

2018: A year of adjustment

Pet loss becomes a focal point in my life. Hal was my rock. I have experienced the loss of pets in the past but never alone and never for a dog that became very close to me after the death of my wife and his master. My world was upside down once again, and I sought help in the form of a pet loss support group and individual therapy for almost an entire year.

2019 to present:

At the end of this year, I retired from the social services field. I continue to acknowledge, accept, and adapt to what life has to offer.

Acknowledgments

I would like to recognize some of those that have helped, encouraged, and contributed along my journey.

Ellen Perry Berkeley
Frances and Steve Caruano
David Clark
Sister Rose Dvorak
David Etzel
Jon Fuller
John Giblo
Kim Gile
Margaret Gore
Char Hafer
Sylvia Havlish
Gary Hawkins
Mallory Hoffman
Kim Howe
Cindy Hurst
Karen Keiser
Brenda Keller
Gregory King
Jennilu King
John Kreiser
Aimee LaPorte
Kevin Lash
Carla Lund
Dave McCormick
Wendy Moore
Kathy Kerper-Morgan
Amanda (Murgido) Morin

Jim Morin
Beth Newman
Anne Nuss
David Parenti
Glenn Petro
Jack and Carol Roach
Kelly O'Neill Rossi
Greg Schweitzer
Willa Scott
Tom Simek
Doug Suereth
Debra Thompson
Lorraine Van Luvender
Rachel Wagenmuth
Cheryl and Darryl Weinhold
Gale Withers
Linda Wrightstone
Raymond Zdradzinski

About the Author

Dominic Murgido has degrees in criminal justice, instructed college courses as an adjunct faculty member, and is a master coffee roaster. He had careers in retail loss prevention and social services. He founded a bereavement support group, *sudSSpirit*, a few years after the sudden unexpected death of his wife. He publishes a quarterly newsletter of the same name. Besides being a grief advocate who provides support and solace to those who are grieving the sudden unexpected death of their spouse or significant other, Dominic is also a writer and speaker. He resides in Pennsylvania.